Spying in America in the Post 9/11 World

Recent Titles in
The Changing Face of War

Spying in America in the Post 9/11 World

Domestic Threat and the Need for Change

Ronald A. Marks

The Changing Face of War
James Jay Carafano, Series Editor

 PRAEGER

AN IMPRINT OF ABC-CLIO, LLC
Santa Barbara, California • Denver, Colorado • Oxford, England

Library of Congress Cataloging-in-Publication Data

Marks, Ronald A.
   Spying in America in the post 9/11 world : domestic threat and the need for change / Ronald A. Marks.
       p. cm. — (Changing face of war)
   Includes bibliographical references and index.
   ISBN 978-0-313-39141-5 (hard copy : alk. paper) — ISBN 978-0-313-39142-2 (e-book) 1. Intelligence service—United States. 2. Civil rights—United States. I. Title.
   JK468.I6M411   2010
   327.1273—dc22   2010031247

ISBN: 978-0-313-39141-5
EISBN: 978-0-313-39142-2

14   13   12   11   10   1   2   3   4   5

This book is also available on the World Wide Web as an eBook.
Visit www.abc-clio.com for details.

Praeger
An Imprint of ABC-CLIO, LLC

ABC-CLIO, LLC
130 Cremona Drive, P.O. Box 1911
Santa Barbara, California 93116-1911

This book is printed on acid-free paper (∞)

Manufactured in the United States of America

Contents

Introduction

One of the challenges of age is your ever-growing memory. Sometimes faulty and seen through rose colored glasses—at other times, those memories are stark and filled with darkness and fear.

I am a child of the Cold War against the Soviet Union. One of my starker memories is when I sat in my grade school hallways during the 1962 Cuban Missile Crisis wondering exactly what would happen if a nuclear bomb hit Portland, Oregon. The pictures on television always showed the mushroom cloud shape and the devastation that followed. No one got around to discussing the fallout and radiation sickness afterward. Still, this time of fear passed. I grew up and moved to Washington, D.C., joined the CIA, and watched the Soviets fade into the dustbin of history.

I am saying this because, while I take the issue of Islamic terrorism seriously, I believe we need to gain some perspective on this threat. Living in Washington, you tend to be surrounded by experts and other types who spend all day thinking about problems. They become justifiably obsessed by these problems. In the case of homeland security, thousands of people are now experts on various subjects that range broadly from things like "risk management" to how to detect body heat crossing a borderline.

Still, speaking as an old Cold Warrior, I believe we need to get some perspective on our enemy and see what our proportional response should be. Let me rephrase it this way: Until Islamic terrorists lay their hands on 1,500 intercontinental ballistic missiles and can destroy every major American city in fifteen minutes, I think we are ill-advised to declare total war on them.

That being said, we are dealing with some very dangerous vipers. They would like to kill us and establish their own perverse form of Islam worldwide. They are also bringing the war to our shores for the first time since the British did so in the War of 1812.

As I write this in midyear 2010, we are apparently on the cusp of a new, Islamic terrorist–related strategy. The use of weapons of mass destruction is moving to a more tactical level. Current trends in terrorist tactics, according to experts, seem to be leaning toward the use of the "singleton"—an individual who is a lone actor and seems to be outside of any organization. "The new terrorist model might be lightly trained individuals deployed as quickly as possible in hopes they succeed," says Juan Zarate, senior adviser in the Transnational Threat Project at the Center for Strategic and International Studies.[1]

On Christmas Day 2009, Umar Farouk Abdul Mutallab, a Nigerian citizen, boarded Northwest Airlines Flight 253 in Amsterdam headed to Detroit. He checked through a relatively lax security and boarded the plane with minimum hassle. Umar had no luggage and had bought his ticket with cash. He went through light screening at the airport, the heavy-duty scanner sitting unused near the gate.

Over the Atlantic, he attempted to light eighty grams of explosives contained in his underwear—enough to blow a hole in the side of the plane and kill all aboard. Thanks to a combination of his ineptness with the fuse and some alert passengers, a tragedy was averted. A video of his training in Yemen later surfaced, showing his training by Al Qaeda in the Arabian Peninsula.[2]

Less than six months later, Faisal Shazad, a native of Pakistan and U.S. citizen living in Bridgeport, Connecticut, attempted to explode/detonate a car bomb in Times Square, New York.[3] Again, thanks to alert citizens and some inept bomb-arming techniques, the bomber was captured. However, while captured a day and a half after the event, Faisal was literally on a plane out the country when he was detained and arrested.[4] A Pakistani Taliban group claimed responsibility for his training and plot.

These incidents served as a stark reminder of both the danger of "lone wolf" terrorists and the fear many of us had after the creation at the federal level of such entities as the Director of National Intelligence (DNI), the National Counterterrorism Center (NCTC), and the Department of Homeland Security (DHS)—that it would be ordinary, observant citizens and local police that would face the terrorists on their own, and the Feds would be backup. And a growing section of the public, and even President Obama, is frustrated by the federal performance.[5]

BUDGET AND PEOPLE ARE NOT THE PROBLEM

It is not as though the Federal government has not tried. If you look at the open budget numbers provided by the DNI since 9/11, you could roughly estimate an expenditure on U.S. intelligence in excess of some $400 billion dollars. Again, by public numbers, this is likely nearly twice what it was in the 1990's. And personnel also seemed to have doubled. Throw in on top of that $40 billion per year for the DHS—well that's what we call real money even by Washington standards.[6,7]

Still, the Underwear Bomber was stopped not by the system devised to protect us. Instead, a few diligent passengers stopped him on a jet traveling at 40,000 feet over the ocean. Bumbling bomb skills and alert citizens stopped another terrorist. So, with much egg on many faces–those who knew about him like NCTC, the Department of State, the Central Intelligence Agency (CIA), and others–the inquiries begin and the system is again revamped and questioned. The American public, forever skeptical of government, is once again shaking its head wondering why they cannot get it right.

I understand the skepticism of the American public. As a thirty-year intelligence professional, I must admit a little more sympathy for the people and the system involved. Sometimes knowing a lot about a system makes you a prisoner of it. In my case, I hope and believe that is not true.

What I do believe is old ideas; faulty bureaucracy and ill-conceived public perceptions fundamentally flaw the current system of doing domestic intelligence in the United States. As the old Ringo Starr song says, "you know, it don't come easy." And it (domestic intelligence) ain't easy for a number of reasons that we will get into in this book.

Another reason I am writing this book is to frame the issues of gathering domestic intelligence in an era where the separation of national boundaries is nearly meaningless. The practitioner, student, and those generally interested in foreign policy and domestic law enforcement issues knows this now more than ever. And, in addition to land, sea and air, we add the dimension of cyber-space—a vast frontier itself owned and governed by no one.

And, finally, I write this book because intelligence, domestic and international, is the guard on the fence of our country. I would hope we would do all we could to help that guard protect our lives and the freedoms we have worked so hard to build over 200 years. I am no ideologue—I like to think of myself as a pragmatist who is trying to frame the problem and then search out a solution, knowing that solution will need to adjust and stretch over time and circumstance.

DISSECTING THE CHALLENGE

One of the challenges in any effort to debate and improve a process is to understand it. We live in an age of the quick sound bite and instant glib analysis. Ideologues wish to score political points, not make progress. This book and its author will brook none of that nonsense.

First, let's look at the fundamentals of intelligence. In many minds, it is the realm of James Bond and Matt Damon. If it were only so sexy! Intelligence is the collection, analysis, and distribution of information that is put in context. The idea that intelligence is a predictor has always been specious based simply on what it is. Foreign policy and law enforcement are most often about making a case with evidence. Intelligence is about anecdote and inference. In short, there is rarely a piece of actionable intelligence.

Not once in the more than thirty years that I have devoted to this game did I hear anyone say, for instance, Joe Blow is going to blow himself up on a street corner in downtown Exville at 2 pm this afternoon. No, more likely, you will get three or four pieces of information. First, someone of varying reliability has said there may be a Joe-like character. Second, he is headed to somewhere in the U.S., maybe you get a city name. Third, he is interested in doing something bad like a bombing or shooting. Then, if you are an analyst of this material, collected from four or five sources, you hope to assemble the pieces in to some kind of order—if you can find the pieces to begin with and if you have the time to do so.

Second, I am also going to explain the multi-headed Hydra know as American intelligence. It is referred to as a community. As we will discover, this community is a loose agglomeration of entities spread through the U.S. government and, even after a few legislative fixes, it is still loosely overseen by both the executive and legislative branches. I will also try to tackle the "new intelligence community," which includes organizations at the federal level and the state and local levels. They range from Customs to Border Patrol to the thousands of local "first responders" who are now a part of the intelligence gathering and using process.

Third, I will discuss the challenge of the present threat to the United States—inside and outside the country. Under the best of circumstances, the threat defines the gathering of intelligence, and gathering intelligence helps define the threat. But, even after eight years of collection and analysis, we are still having trouble defining the threat. And in this lies one of the key challenges of domestic intelligence: the concept of risk assessment and risk management. The first understands the nature of the challenge and its ever shifting dimensions and realistically assesses the chance of events and strategies occurring. The latter concept focuses on resources; how much can you sensibly afford to spend on risks and which ones should you tackle. The first is the bailiwick of intelligence. The latter is the territory of the policymaker. One hopes the first supports the second; when it does not, you have trouble.

Still, we need to be realistic about what we can and cannot defend. We could spend the entire national treasury and more trying to defend ourselves. East Germany, during the Cold War, had an estimated five percent of its population spying on the other 95 percent. And still, information and people escaped to the West.[8]

Good risk management by policymakers focuses on the most likely risks against the most likely targets and puts manpower and material resources against them. This sounds simple, but it is not. What you protect enters the realm of politics. Eighty-five percent of the American infrastructure (e.g., power plants) are held in private hands.

Fourth, we must look at the issue of collecting intelligence within the United States. As mentioned before, Americans have a mixed view of government and a very mixed view of intelligence gathering within its borders.

It all starts with the Enlightenment and one of its children, the U.S. Constitution. The latter is more than a document. Its very creation tapped the deepest root of the American psyche. We fundamentally do not trust government. Born of the Enlightenment and reinforced under British governance and the American Revolution against them, Americans developed a base document for our governance that makes no bones about separation of powers into definable and countervailing forces. We have three branches of government, two of which involved direct election by the people. We have state's rights versus federal rights. And we have specific rules of order governing both with a judicial branch to play umpire. As a friend of mine says, the difference between the British and us is we are citizens and they are subjects.

Domestic intelligence collection is about trusting government. Can we allow our government to be intrusive in our lives and not end up the worse for it? Who is collecting the information? What kind of oversight is in place, and will this oversight protect us sufficiently from abuse? And who is seeing and holding this information?

The historic track record of American domestic intelligence is not covered with glory. True, the Federal Bureau of Investigation (FBI) did a good job of uncovering Axis spies in the United States during World War II. However, its leader J. Edgar Hoover carried on a hunt against communist influence and "agents of influence" in the 1950s and 1960s that could be charitably described as excessive. Congress and the FBI succumbed to a communist paranoia in this period that ruined many a life and left those reviewing this period perplexed. For every Rosenberg case, there were files compiled on such national dangers as Jane Fonda, John Lennon, and Dr. Martin Luther King. And we found federal players supposedly devoted to overseas activities such as CIA and the U.S. Army intelligence collecting information on college campuses and in the streets of America.

The final blowup—the Mrs. O'Leary's cow that kicked over the domestic intelligence lantern—was the Watergate scandal. President Richard Nixon used people in the White House to spy on enemies. He was found out, and all the spying activities that had gone on without oversight came tumbling down. The bad taste from that period remains to this day in the collective mouth of Americans.

Still, the circumstances of today do not reflect the reality of thirty years ago. This is not just about the laws that have changed since 9/11 to lower the steel curtain arranged between domestic and international intelligence. It is about an increasing fear that Americans have been whistling through the graveyard regarding domestic terrorism.

A spate of recent events from Fort Hood to U.S. citizens volunteering to participate in radical Islamic activities has made Americans painfully aware that our inclusiveness and willingness to tolerate all attitudes is not enough. We dismissed the Europeans for ghettoizing and isolating their Muslin minorities. No longer are we "safe" from domestic terrorists. But what rights must we surrender to stop these actions? In times of war, America has gone to extremes. But is this terrorism really war or something else? If it is something else, what rules apply?

Fifth, we have yet another challenge to deal with: the bureaucracy of the U.S. government and state and local enforcement and intelligence organizations. As we said before, Americans love decentralization of government, and we have been effective at separating police and intelligence authorities. In the United States, we have sixteen federal intelligence organizations. In addition, the FBI, Drug Enforcement Administration, Customs, and a list of others in the federal law enforcement bureaucracy are also collecting information for their purposes. And, last but hardly least, we have 17,600 state, local, and tribal law authorities doing information collection and policing. They range in size from one person to 30,000 people.[9]

In an effort by some local groups to collect information and coordinate intelligence locally and with the federal government, more than seventy "fusion centers" now exist around the country.[10] From the beginning, these centers have contained a mix of local police, FBI, DHS, and CIA officers collecting information, doing analysis, and trying to engage the federal authorities to receive and exchange comparable information and intelligence. Training and communication for these fusion centers have been spotty, and there has been no centralized control or standardization of them.

Passing the information and intelligence collected has not been easy. We have had numerous message systems for passing information and a laundry list of compartmentalized information types classified to various levels of access. If domestic intelligence for both the federal and local levels were an organ of the human body, it would be the human lung: thousands of little sacs of information and controls and organizations in little compartments. At least, the human lung functions with central muscle control, which is more than can be said for the current system.

Sixth, we will look outside the United States to another country with similar experiences and law. We need to ask the question: Is this messy system of protecting our homeland something that others experience, or are we truly unique? The answer is both yes and no. For the sake of argument in this book, I intend to look at the system closest to us by law and heritage, the United Kingdom. When there is a discussion of how well things work between law enforcement and intelligence, many experts point to the United Kingdom. These experts insinuate rather blithely that what America really needs is an MI-5. They usually do so without having a clue about what MI-5 really does or understanding how the British system works in some ways that simply are not possible in the United States at this time.

And, seventh, we will look at whether our civil liberties can be maintained in the face of larger and more intrusive American domestic intelligence. The main portion of that concern over what does and does not work in America comes down to the fundamental, Constitutional delineation of government power versus civil liberties. The Founding Fathers made no bones about not trusting government. It is the basis of every child's education and the DNA in American bones. This attitude is also running headlong into the ugly realities of life post-9/11. And, sometimes in the fast, the shibboleth is temporarily overrun by fear.

Ultimately, the question of preserving our liberties is determined in the short and long runs by what we are facing in terms of threat. Is this war against a sworn enemy, a non-nation state? Or is this police action against a group of thugs? The answer leads to a core issue of domestic intelligence: How far should we go to protect ourselves?

Sadly, the answer is likely that Islamic terrorism is both war and police action. In physics, scientists talk about the "plasma" state between water and gas. This engagement we are now in is a plasma state of action—it is neither fish nor fowl. Thus, we have swung back and forth since 9/11, and this trend is not likely to stop.

SOLUTIONS

This book is also about solutions. One of the more troublesome aspects of living in the fishbowl of Washington, D.C., is that it is full of smart people. Many of these smart people show how smart they are by pointing out the problems. Well, as Jack Nicholson said in the movie *As Good As It Gets*, "I am drowning here, and you are pointing out the color of the water."

I believe the next steps in developing American domestic intelligence is to break out the most troubling parts and see what can be done with them. A word of warning: None of this is going to be clean and solve all the problems. A further word of warning: the American public and its politicians need to understand that this is a system that will sometimes fail, no matter what you do. Risk management is about managing and reducing risk, not eliminating risk.

I will take a look at simplifying the complex bureaucracy through which information flows and does not flow. I will also talk about keeping the people involved in the oversight of the process. Our liberties are too important to be left to the bureaucrats alone. Finally, I will recommend how we keep the public informed in a way that gives them insight into the process of domestic intelligence while balancing the ability to keep the secrets necessary to defend our country.

As I said, none of this will be easy, but it is necessary. We have not survived 230 years only to surrender ourselves to our fears and the threats of our enemies. And yet, the U.S. Constitution is not a suicide pact. The American people know this, but they must be engaged in debate before we go too far down the road. Otherwise, the backlash will be strong and not necessarily in our longer-term interests.

1
Chapter

What Constitutes Intelligence?

Before we launch into the issue of domestic intelligence, it is important to understand exactly what we are discussing. In short, we need to know the following things: What is intelligence? How is it collected? How is it composed into analysis? How is it presented to the people who use it, the so-called "policymakers?" What is domestic intelligence? And how has it been used?

Intelligence is based on data and information. By definition, a piece of data is a fact. Information is the imposition of structure around data. Both are pieces of what the professionals call raw intelligence. They need to be mined out of the vast universe in which data and information exist. Then they are put into context—some frame of reference to the rest of the world—by an expert, an analyst, whether they are working for the CIA or for a large firm like Exxon.

Let's take a simple example of how the process works. My computer has access to the Internet, which now stores terabytes of data. Data is a thing. For example, data can be a statement: there is a chair in the kitchen. Information defines the thing: the wooden chair is in the kitchen. Intelligence provides context: the wooden chair is in the kitchen in this house and is sometimes used for dining. Intelligence analysis takes intelligence and moves it one step further. Analysis tries to frame this fact in an overall view using other pieces of intelligence to predict an outcome. For instance, the chair in the kitchen, sometimes used for dining, on a number of occasions in the past has been used as a step ladder when a light blows out; next time the light blows out, the owner will likely use it as a step ladder."

As we enter the second decade of the 21st century, gaining access to data and information is no longer a problem. Within the last decade in particular, we access much of it by electronic means either through intranets (within a given community of interest) or the Internet (i.e., the World Wide Web).

And we access it with ease. We have PCs, cell phones, laptops, blackberries, etc. It still amazes me that the very laptop I am typing this book on can reach into cyberspace. I have access to email systems, communities like Facebook and Twitter, wikis, newspapers, blogs, web sites, and so on.

For the analyst, however, the Internet and the explosion of data and information are both a boon and a bane. The analyst needs data and information, of which there is plenty. And here comes the downside: they also need to sort through it. Many software firms are now making a great deal of money selling the latest and greatest data mining software, such as Google, to sort through the ever-expanding cyber universe.

Another challenge to the intelligence analyst is that today's policymakers—the people who make the decisions—also have access to the same kind of information. Policymakers are now also analysts in their own right. For instance, President Obama, after much handwringing by the security people, got his Blackberry; this is but one window to the Internet world. He also has a computer he uses. The man is connected to cyberspace.

This rapid development is quite a shock to analysts both inside government and in the private sector. In the old days of pre-Internet intelligence analysis, an analyst was someone who had unique access to data and information. The Cold War CIA was a tribute to unique access based on clandestine gathering of information. Much of that information today is available to anyone. How good that information is and how good the analysis on which it is based is a story we will discuss later in this chapter.

WHAT IS INTELLIGENCE?

So what exactly is so special about intelligence done for the government? And what do the experts have to say? As usual, expert opinions abound, but they all come back to the same principals of intelligence.

Dr. Mark Lowenthal, one of the premier experts on American intelligence, defines it this way: "Intelligence is the process by which specific types of information important to national security are requested, collected, analyzed, and provided to policymakers; the products of that process; the safeguarding of those process and this information by counterintelligence (CI) activities; and the carrying out of operations as requested by lawful authorities."[1] In other words, intelligence is about the synthesis of data and information and passing it to people who can use it.

Another intelligence expert, Jack Davis, outlines the idea further though with an eye only on foreign intelligence. Davis says, "Intelligence analysis is the process of providing objective and effective support to help U.S. policymakers, by means of information on and assessments on events overseas, to carry out their mission of formulating and implementing national security policy.[2]

As for making predictions, what all policymakers desire of intelligence—the bottom line—is best expressed by Robert Clark, "Describing a past event is not intelligence analysis, it is history. True intelligence analysis is always predictive."[3]

The history of intelligence is often written on its ability to predict or otherwise lay out scenarios for the future. Still, while there are uses for intelligence, it also has its limits.

THE USES AND LIMITS OF INTELLIGENCE

When former Assistant to the President for Homeland Security Frank Cilluffo and I wrote an article in the Washington Quarter on the use and limits of foreign and domestic intelligence, we were both painfully aware that intelligence is a tool and not a cure-all.[4] Intelligence involves the understanding of the motivations, the thoughts and the plans of one's opponents. Multidisciplinary intelligence, including insights into the cultures and mindsets of terrorist organizations, is crucial to providing indications and warnings of possible attacks and is vital to illuminating key vulnerabilities that can be exploited and leveraged to prevent, preempt, and disrupt terrorist activities before they occur.[5]

We also noted that analysts are estimators, not clairvoyants. In the best of circumstances, a well-trained analyst cannot read an opponent's mind. Analysts can explain a trend or understand a motivation, but they will not know everything. In a world of compartmentalized cells—perhaps consisting of three or four people—data and information gathered for intelligence analysis will be circumstantial, not conclusive.[6] One of the best examples of the limits of any analyst and analytical capability is the famous Presidential Daily Brief (PDB) of 6 August 2001 entitled, "Bin Laden Determined to Strike in U.S." First, however, a little about the why and the wherefore of the PDB itself.

In analytical circles, the PDB is the Rolls Royce of analysis. It is what all analysts aspire to produce; including me in my short stint as an analyst. The PDB is meant for the President and his few select advisors who have access to this most classified of information.

The PDB is intended to provide the president of the United States with new international intelligence warranting attention and analysis of sensitive international situations. The prototype of the PDB was called the President's Intelligence Check List; the first was produced by Richard Lehman at the direction of Huntington D. Sheldon on 17 June 1961. The CIA produced the first PDB for Lyndon B. Johnson on 1 December 1964.[7]

Figure 1.1

Bin Ladin Determined To Strike in US

Clandestine, foreign government, and media reports indicate Bin Ladin since 1997 has wanted to conduct terrorist attacks in the US. Bin Ladin implied in US television interviews in 1997 and 1998 that his followers would follow the example of World Trade Center bomber Ramzi Yousef and "bring the fighting to America."

After US missile strikes on his base in Afghanistan in 1998, Bin Ladin told followers he wanted to retaliate in Washington, according to a ▬▬▬▬▬ service.

An Egyptian Islamic Jihad (EIJ) operative told an ▬▬▬ service at the same time that Bin Ladin was planning to exploit the operative's access to the US to mount a terrorist strike.

The millennium plotting in Canada in 1999 may have been part of Bin Ladin's first serious attempt to implement a terrorist strike in the US. Convicted plotter Ahmed Ressam has told the FBI that he conceived the idea to attack Los Angeles International Airport himself, but that Bin Ladin lieutenant Abu Zubaydah encouraged him and helped facilitate the operation. Ressam also said that in 1998 Abu Zubaydah was planning his own US attack.

Ressam says Bin Ladin was aware of the Los Angeles operation.

Although Bin Ladin has not succeeded, his attacks against the US Embassies in Kenya and Tanzania in 1998 demonstrate that he prepares operations years in advance and is not deterred by setbacks. Bin Ladin associates surveilled our Embassies in Nairobi and Dar es Salaam as early as 1993, and some members of the Nairobi cell planning the bombings were arrested and deported in 1997.

Al-Qa'ida members—including some who are US citizens—have resided in or traveled to the US for years, and the group apparently maintains a support structure that could aid attacks. Two al-Qa'ida members found guilty in the conspiracy to bomb our Embassies in East Africa were US citizens, and a senior EIJ member lived in California in the mid-1990s.

A clandestine source said in 1998 that a Bin Ladin cell in New York was recruiting Muslim-American youth for attacks.

We have not been able to corroborate some of the more sensational threat reporting, such as that from a ▬▬▬▬▬ *service in 1998 saying that Bin Ladin wanted to hijack a US aircraft to gain the release of "Blind Shaykh" 'Umar 'Abd al-Rahman and other US-held extremists.*

continued

For the President Only
6 August 2001

— Nevertheless, FBI information since that time indicates patterns of
    suspicious activity in this country consistent with preparations for
    hijackings or other types of attacks, including recent surveillance of
    federal buildings in New York.

The FBI is conducting approximately 70 full field investigations
throughout the US that it considers Bin Ladin–related. CIA and the
FBI are investigating a call to our Embassy in the UAE in May saying
that a group of Bin Ladin supporters was in the US planning attacks
with explosives.

When you tour the CIA Museum, you can see the PDB in its various forms. Sometimes it comes in a loose-leaf notebook binder, and at other times it is bound. Always on the front are the words "Presidential Daily Brief." Inside is a collection of articles written by a staff devoted to culling intelligence materials of such importance to be presented to the President. The PDB is typically presented to the president in the morning. Clearly, it a document that does not contain immediate news, but one that tries to present it in some context. Presenters of the PDB and the how the presidents read the PDB have differed over time, depending upon the president.

On the latter point, a great deal of bureaucratic bloodshed goes into face time with the president. As you can imagine, the PDB would allow such access as some White House staff might now want. The prime determinant in this exercise is the president's National Security Advisor. A political employee, the National Security Advisor is the guardian at the gate, and some guard more strongly than others.

For example, Dr. David Young, who served as the personal assistant to Henry Kissinger while he was National Security Advisor to Richard Nixon, reported that Kissinger briefed the president with the PDB himself. Director of Central Intelligence (DCI) Richard Helms rarely saw the President. This practice was also followed by President Carter's National Security Advisor Zbig Brezinski.

In the George H.W. Bush Administration, the president (a former head of Central Intelligence) liked to read the "book" with a briefer on hand, of whom the president could ask questions. National Security Advisor Brent Scowcroft had no problem allowing this because Robert Gates, Scowcroft's former deputy, was heading CIA. Under President George H.W. Bush, unanswered questions were then relayed back to PDB staff and answered as soon as possible.

President George W. Bush enjoyed the company of his DCI George Tenet, who tried to present the PDB often, or Michael Morrell, a favored head of the PDB staff (and current number two at CIA). Together with Condoleezza Rice, the PDB was briefed and discussions ensued about articles of the day.

The 6 August article was a typical PDB article. Rumors had been swirling for some time that there would be an attack by Al Qaeda somewhere in the world, possibly the United States.[8] An article was commissioned and the redacted results are shown here (Figure 1.1).[9]

The language of the piece is most striking to the outsider. The reader will note in the first sentence that the analysts include a lot of sources but is willing to say only "indicate" and "implied" as a judgment about the potential attack and Bin Laden's intentions. Continuing on through the piece, the analysts also carefully lay out what certain sources said and what could be corroborated in certain instances. And, finally, the analysts seem to conclude that hijackings were a possibility and New York City might be a target. It never drew the two conclusions closely together as there simply was no intelligence evidence of it.

The challenge of any intelligence article, like the above, is that intelligence remains anecdotal versus evidentiary. It is a world of the implied and the potential. Part of this is that analysts, like anyone else, hate to get it wrong. Part of it remains that analysts ultimately can only work with what they have.

It is on this latter point that much of the challenge rests. I would not let analysts off the hook for being too cautious or not imaginative enough. But I would also say that the collectors of information can be equally unimaginative and sometimes simply overwhelmed with data.

Speaking as a former collector of information at the national level, I know the volume can be staggering. But much depends on how you aim your targeting. And you must also overcome a culture that says collecting some of this information is "cop work," (i.e., "This is law enforcement, like the FBI or state and local police, let them work it out.").

From a collector's standpoint as well, how willing are you to get close to dangerous groups like Bin Laden or the Taliban? How willing are you to get close to American terrorists and their overseas contacts? And, as a collector, how can you avoid going over the line between intelligence gathering and the fear of the "police state?"

WHAT BOTHERS AMERICANS ABOUT DOMESTIC INTELLIGENCE?

The key to understanding the basis of U.S. discomfort over domestic intelligence issues lies in both its connection to the new information age and our heritage of centuries past. The American psyche has deep roots.

Since the Treaty of Westphalia in 1648, the world has defined itself in terms of national borders, as nation-states. France is France. Japan is Japan. South Africa is South Africa. Even the extensive colonies controlled by the colonial powers of the 19th century divided themselves into nations. The nation was a part of a person's identity.

Clearly, there are other things that defined a person. Ideology always plays a role. Religious movements like Christianity, Islam, etc., have a strong identity. Pan-national movements such as communism, anarchism, and others also have a strong hold on people around the world. Whatever the ideology, in the past it was defined by where you lived, land, sea, and air. Travel was not easy and took time. Communication means could be relatively controlled by the state. Borders, while not totally secure, gave some sense of stability to nation-states.

The late 20th and early 21st centuries are defined by the weakening of the nation-state context. Physical travel can put anyone anywhere in the world in less than 24 hours, and the Internet and the cyberspace within it allow instant movement of ideas and the creation of "worlds" and communities of interest without any physical boundaries. All in all, these advances have torn down borders and made domestic intelligence a greater priority for all nations. For the United States, the world's remaining nation-state superpower, it has been a very rude awakening. Our enemies are no longer at our borders—they are within.

So what is this domestic intelligence that is so upsetting to the American body politic? Definitions of domestic intelligence today abound, but the simplest and most complete definition is from the mind of intelligence aficionado Judge Richard Posner: "Domestic national security intelligence ("domestic intelligence" for short) is intelligence concerning threats of major, politically motivated violence, or of equally grievous harm to national security, mounted within the nation's territorial limits, whether by international terrorists, homegrown terrorists, or spies or saboteurs employed by foreign governments."[10]

Ignoring the ever-present question that one man's terrorist is another man's freedom fighter, Posner's definition strikes at a fact with which America is coming to grips: By what means do we gather information against terrorists who may live within our borders and are perhaps our own citizens, who needs to be involved, what are we protecting, and how do we protect the very civil liberties of our society while we do so?

THE MECHANICS OF SPYING

Much as been made of spying over the years that is both legend and fantasy. The first legend is that of the derring-do of James Bond, master British spy. He flies around the world and collects information and women, and leaves death to enemies in his wake. Thrilling, but not even close to the reality of the tight, confined world of collecting information from humans and giving that information to those who need it to make policy judgments.

Another fantasy involves that of Big Brother. Partially spawn by justifiable paranoia of what the State will do with information collected on individuals, this fantasy sees the State like George Orwell's "1984." The State sees and knows all. The aforementioned East Germans had files on some six million of their eighteen million people and may have had some 800,000 people involved in some form of spying; however, they are no longer here.[11] Even the hellhole of North Korea cannot prevent its people from collecting information from the outside world, even by cell phone nowadays.[12]

So what is the reality of spying? How is the information collected, reviewed, processed, and presented to the policymakers? The intelligence cycle, as it is called, is the same around the world and works the same whether done overseas or at home. It starts with how you collect the information.

A WORLD OF INTS

The first step in the Intelligence Cycle is collection. You need to have information on which to base your judgments. The collection of intelligence (and you'll notice this is used interchangeably with intelligence) comes down to three basic methods (INTs) plus a relatively new one: from humans, from signals, from pictures, and from open sources. In the parlance of the trade, these three classic means are known as INTs: HUMINT (human intelligence), SIGINT (signals intelligence), GEOINT (imagery and other visual intelligence), and OSINT (open-source intelligence gathered more openly than the others), newly coming into acceptance.

HUMINT is the classic, millennia-old spy collection method. The joke in the trade is it is the "second oldest profession." Basically, it is humans collecting information from other humans. Sometimes, the information is of a political, economic or military nature; who in a government wants to do what. Other times, it can involve the planting of devices that collect information electronically. In those ways, James Bond's tactics are about right.

SIGINT has been around since the invention of the telegraph, though some claim that observing flag signals from ship to ship is the earliest example. It is exactly what it sounds like; someone intercepts and translates messages sent either openly or clandestinely. On the latter point, if the message is sent clandestinely, you either find the secret way it is being sent or decode it if it is hidden in some kind of code.

GEOINT used to be called IMINT or Imagery Intelligence. This INT was originally about pictures, but has expanded in the 21st century. Primarily starting in World War I, GEOINT was simply overhead shots taken of battlefields and gun emplacements. During the Cold War, GEOINT was essentially the same thing, only performed with much more expensive and complex tools like high-flying U-2 spy planes and satellites. Collection remains the same today, though the material now collected goes into the creation of detailed maps for soldiers or other types of topographic material.

The relatively new INT is OSINT. OSINT could be as simple as collecting information from newspapers, books, or radio stations. It might also include gathering information from college papers or journals. What has added new impetus to OSINT is the Internet. The world of cyberspace is filled with terabytes of information expanding at an ever-increasing rate—even those who know the subject well can only guess.[13] This information may be held in blogs or web sites, shared on Twitter or other new social sites, or simply sent back and forth in e-mails and text messages.

THE IMPORTANCE OF HUMINT

While I have my personal biases, many intelligence experts consider human intelligence collection to be the key INT. As the Weapons of Mass Destruction (WMD) Commission stated in its report, "Human intelligence serves policymakers by providing a unique window into the target's most guarded intentions, plans and programs."[14] History is filled with stories of famed spies. For example, Soviet Colonel Oleg Penkovskiy saved the United States during the Cuban missile crisis by sharing Moscow's intentions with the Kennedy administration. A number of people helped nail down the nuclear proliferation efforts of Pakistani scientist A.Q. Khan.

So what is human intelligence and how do you collect it? Well, in many ways you do it every day. In the parlance of the business, you are spotting, targeting, assessing, validating, and recruiting.

For instance, let's say you are interested in hiring an assistant. You call your friends and business associates to find out who might be available. You might place an advertisement on Craigslist.org or in the newspaper. You are trying to spot potential candidates. Through your spotting efforts, you receive a pile of names and resumes. You start to break them down by the qualities you want in an assistant. For example, you might want someone who can manage the office, assist you with your calendar and appointments, answer the phones, etc. Maybe you want them to have a certain level of education or experience. After the sort, you find several likely candidates. You have targeted the people you wish to interview.

The next stage is the interview. Let's say you have three people with whom you want to talk. You bring them into your office for a meeting. You talk for a half hour or so about their background and interests. You are also trying to get a gauge of whether this person can really do the job and whether you can get along with them. This is assessing potential hires. You are validating whether their skill set is what you need.

Finally, you decide on the candidate you want to hire. You call them or send them a formal offer letter. The letter lays out the terms and conditions of their employment. You tell them what the salary and benefits are, and you let them know what duties are expected of them. You might still have to negotiate a bit, but in essence you have recruited them to work for you.

The recruitment of spies—assets in the parlance of the trade—is the key part of your job. Without assets, there is no chance to gather any information of any value. You might speak to them in a less formal way before the recruitment. They might even provide you some good information, but recruiting solidifies the bond between the case officer (the controller of the asset) and the asset themselves. It is a contract in word and deed. An important factor is that it takes time to do this and time to feel comfortable that your asset is providing the right kind of information.

As you might imagine, the process of finding assets and collecting information from them can be troublesome. First of all, you are not the only person out there spying. There are other countries and groups trying to collect information, sometimes about you and your country, and they will send people to you to provide false or misleading information.

This is the world of CI. You are always trying to see whether the asset you recruited is trustworthy. Are they providing you good information? Are they working for someone else? It is not a game that inspires trust; as the old Russian proverb goes, "trust but verify."

Another challenge you face is what access assets have to information. You want information about things that you do not know about. You want information about what the leadership of a country or group is thinking. If you could see into the mind of Kim Jong-Il of North Korea or Osama Bin Laden, that would greatly help the cause of America.

However, these groups are not easy to penetrate. They are called "hard targets." Sometimes it is a question of language. Your ability to speak decent Arabic will influence what kind of assets you can recruit. This skill will also allow you to detect the nuances in what they are saying to you, to ask the second and third question, not just the first.

Other times hard targets are what they sound like, hard places to get into or fade into in a way that will avoid detection. It is unlikely as an American that you will cross the North Korea border without more than a few questions. Even if you do, they are going to follow you and discover everyone with whom you speak. Getting close to the leadership would be near impossible.

You also can't waltz into an Al Qaeda cell and ask them if they are planning any bombings today. Many of these groups are based on personal or family connections. It takes a long time to make them feel comfortable with you, and even longer to get them to discuss what they are up to. Not impossible, but damn hard.

One way to get around this direct approach is to find a third party to go in and collect the information. As obvious as this may be, you have to trust them (obviously) and you have to trust that the information they get is trustworthy (not always so easy.) A classic example of where this "third party" business goes wrong is an asset, code named "Curveball," that the Germans offered to us in advance of the Second Gulf War. According to the Germans, this asset had excellent access to the senior levels of the Saddam Hussein government. He also had information on the Iraq program for producing WMDs such as chemical and biological weapons as well as nuclear weapons.

As the WMD report reminds us, this lack of direct U.S. control of the asset did not work. The asset flat-out lied to our German friends, and we then included the information in our analysis to the Bush Administration on Iraqi capabilities. It was a textbook case of not validating the asset or his information.[15]

This leads to another issue: human intelligence, by virtue of the time it takes to make a recruitment and task the asset, is not always capable of turning on a dime when the political requirements change. For instance, while the United States may be concentrating its political concerns on countries in the Middle East, what happens if something occurs in sub-Saharan Africa? Do we have the right people with the right languages in the right places to collect information? If we don't, how fast can we get them and will they be able to collect anything worthwhile and in what time frame?

U.S. HUMINT REDUX

As we will discuss later in the book, the Curveball case led to a number of changes in the structure of the intelligence community (IC) and the 2004 Intelligence Reform and Terrorism Prevention Act (IRTPA).[16] One of the largest changes was who oversaw HUMINT for the entire IC.

As a result of IRTPA, in October 2005, the National Clandestine Service (NCS) was created, effectively renaming the Directorate of Operations. The NCS serves as the clandestine arm of the CIA, i.e., the human intelligence collection wing of the CIA. The head of the service effectively took over the national authority for the coordination, deconfliction, and evaluation of clandestine operations across the U.S. IC.[17]

This NCS coordination job includes, but is not limited to, the FBI, the Diplomatic Security Service, the Defense Intelligence Agency (DIA), the Air Force ISR Agency, the Army Intelligence and Security Command (INSCOM), Marine Corps Intelligence Activity, and the Office of Naval Intelligence.[18] It also includes interacting with the new DNI office, where a full section was devoted to total IC resources going to collection including human intelligence.[19]

HUMINT, like the other INTs, does not stand-alone. It is part of a total process that is known as the Intelligence Cycle.

WHAT IS THE INTELLIGENCE CYCLE?

Having information is one thing. How you process it, make sense out of it, and deliver it to the policymaker is called the intelligence cycle. It is both simple and complex. And while you will get the school solution below, know that the effort is as complex and complicated as the people and the situations that intelligence addresses.

There are five steps that constitute the intelligence cycle.[20, 21]

Planning and Direction

This is management of the entire effort, from identifying the need for data to delivering an intelligence product to a consumer. It is the beginning and the end of the cycle—the beginning because it involves drawing up specific collection requirements, and the end because finished intelligence, which supports policy decisions, generates new requirements.

The whole process depends on guidance from public officials. Policymakers—the president, his aides, the National Security Council, and other major departments and agencies of government—initiate requests for intelligence.

Collection

Collection is the gathering of the raw information needed to produce finished intelligence. There are many sources of information, including open sources such as foreign broadcasts, newspapers, periodicals, and books. Open source reporting is integral to the IC's analytical capabilities. There are also secret sources of information. The IC's operations officers collect such information from agents abroad and from defectors who provide information obtainable in no other way. Technical collection—using electronics and satellite photography—plays an indispensable role in modern intelligence, such as monitoring arms control agreements and providing direct support to military forces.

Processing

Processing involves converting the vast amount of information collected to a form usable by analysts through decryption, language translations, and data reduction.

All-Source Analysis and Production

All-source analysis and production is the conversion of basic information into finished intelligence. It includes integrating, evaluating, and analyzing all available data, which is often fragmentary and even contradictory, and then preparing intelligence products. Analysts, who are subject-matter specialists, consider the information's reliability, validity, and relevance. They integrate data into a coherent whole, put the evaluated information in context, and produce finished intelligence that includes assessments of events and judgments about the implications of the information for the United States.

The IC devotes the bulk of its resources to providing strategic intelligence to policymakers. It performs this important function by monitoring events, warning decision makers about threats to the United States, and forecasting developments. The subjects involved may concern different regions, problems, or personalities in various contexts, political, geographic, economic, military, scientific, or biographic. Current events, capabilities, and future trends are examined.

All-source analysts, at CIA, DIA, and Department of State Bureau of Intelligence and Research (INR) produce numerous written reports, which may be brief notes—one page or less—or lengthy studies. They may involve current intelligence, which is of immediate importance, or long-range assessments. The CIA presents some finished intelligence in oral briefings. All members of the IC also participate in the drafting and production of National Intelligence Estimates, which reflect the collective judgments of the IC.

Dissemination

The last step, which logically feeds into the first, is the distribution of the finished intelligence to the consumers, the same policymakers whose needs initiated the intelligence requirements. Finished intelligence is hand-carried daily to the President and key national security advisers. The policymakers, the recipients of finished intelligence, then make decisions based on the information, and these decisions may lead to the levying of more requirements, thus triggering the intelligence cycle.

THE FEEDBACK LOOP

In its most straightforward way, intelligence begins and ends with the policymaker. This is the person who must make the decisions. Intelligence is used to advise that person, to inform them as they make their decision. To do so, you must know what that policymaker wants and what they need. Given how busy most policymakers are, it comes down to a hit-and-miss game by those intelligence persons in contact with policymaker to "know their customer."

This initial feedback of what the customer needs should first inform the structure of collection. In other words, to collect the information you need to know what kinds of people and things do you need to buy and keep in your system. For instance, if there is strong need to have assets who speak Farsi, you need to recruit officers and analysts who speak Farsi. If you require more and better information from imagery, you need to get better satellites built for you. As you can imagine, the potential delays in this cycle often contribute to some very expensive mistakes or misallocations.

Once you have the means to collect, then logically you go and collect. But, collecting is not always as easy as it sounds. You may have some insight into what you need to collect and the means to do so, but you still have to find the information. The information may be difficult to obtain, such as the inner political workings of North Korea, or so plentiful it is mind-boggling, like the vast world of cyberspace.

Then you need to decide on the most cost effective way of collecting the information. Why would you use a satellite when a human could collect the information far more cheaply? Why would you use a human when a few keys strokes could obtain the information?

So, now you have the information. The next step is to process and exploit it. Processing is like old-fashioned factory work. You may have thousands of pieces of intelligence collected on a given issue. Sometimes it comes in digits. Other times it comes in pixels. Other times it comes in words. The massive volume dictates that you determine first what you have and then send it to the right analytical places to be used.

ANALYSIS AND THE POLICYMAKER

The next "stage" of the intelligence cycle is that of analysis and the analyst. This person needs to be reasonably expert in their field of interest so that they can explain and put into context the intelligence they receive. As you might imagine, the volume of information received by an analyst can be enormous. Even using the best information sorting tools, it is up to the analyst to determine what is needed to provide analysis that will inform the policymaker. The analyst must be able to convey the analysis in a way that it makes sense to the policymaker. The analysis itself is policy neutral. Information is provided and placed into context. The analyst is not a part of the policymaking process.

Finally, where the cycle both begins and ends is the policymaker. This is the person who makes the decisions and on whom final judgments will rest for success or failure. Each one has their own peculiarities in terms of how they receive the information. Some like it in written form; others prefer to be briefed orally or with a slide presentation. In the final analysis, how they use the information is up to them. Sometimes this means interpreting the information in a fashion they want rather than how it is presented. This is the bugaboo of all analysis—the so-called "politicization of intelligence." From a policymaker's standpoint, this means little. The policymaker's greatest fears were best expressed by political and military theorist General Carl Von Clausewitz: "That most intelligence is false, and the effect of fear is to multiply lies and inaccuracies."[22]

As I said before, this is the school solution. The failures of collection and analysis—as well as successes—can fill many books, and we will discuss both later in this book. Still, the ability to move massive amounts of information from collection to the policymaker takes place 365 days a year. That is nearly a miracle in and of itself.

THE CHALLENGE OF SHARING INFORMATION

The intelligence cycle has other challenges in addition to feedback and volume. All four of these INTs, along with the analysis in which they are used, are subject to who needs to know what. Again, in the parlance of the trade, there must be "the need to know" this information before you can see it. For instance, if you are worried about a terrorist cell in Detroit, do you really need to see information about South Korean rice crops?

This "need to know" business becomes very complex very quickly. First, intelligence is always "classified." Governments have been doing this for years, and the United States is no exception. The classification often has to do with the sources of the information and how they were collected. For example, information collected from a spy satellite might be regarded as Top Secret with all kinds of caveats on who is "cleared to see the information." The more sensitive as to source and method, the more highly classified. To receive this information, a person must be cleared through a security background check to be entitled to review this information.

Then there is the issue of intelligence compartmentation. The term compartmentation means not the classification, but who really needs to see it. Again, refer to the previous example. Someone doing terrorist reporting may have the same clearances as the person following terrorist plots in Los Angeles. The question is do they need to share any of this information, and if so, what should be shared?

The challenge of these questions has been made enormously complex in the information age of the 21st century. First, while the classification business is important, what happens when you find out you could get the same information from the Internet or other unclassified means? This so-called OSINT calls for a long look at what classified information is collected and how it is collected. This situation also raises the following difficult question: If an intelligence agent collects it (e.g., CIA), does that make it classified? In other words, is the CIA looking at secret information? If the CIA agent asks a question, does that "spill the beans" to others who may be enemies about the issues we are monitoring?

As you can see, the very mechanics and security aspects of intelligence make it hard to share information readily, and these aspects are now deeply ingrained in the culture of the American intelligence system. Now, comes the issue of CI.

WHO DO YOU TRUST?

When people speak of CI, they speak of its American "founder," James Jesus Angleton. A gaunt, austere man with an Ivy League background and a deeply ingrained alcohol problem, Angleton ruled the world of CI. Many in CIA considered him paranoid, seeking spies where there were none.

While all of this may be true, he also introduced the concept to U.S. intelligence that simply because someone was an American spy did not mean they could be trusted not to turn on their country. Someone who was willing to provide information to you needed to be vetted again and again. As someone once told me, in the spy game, you have persons of mutual interests, but no friends. While this sounds enormously cynical, there has been plenty of evidence to prove Angleton's point.

CI is about determining who is trying to steal what information from you. It is also about determining what people or systems you own might be vulnerable to that theft. CI is a murky business with few clear answers and many, many more questions. This is truly the game of spy versus spy.

CI is deeply ingrained in the American intelligence community, thanks to Angleton and the more than fifty years of dealing with the former Soviet Union. The USSR was a dictatorship and a police state, and the KGB was their internal and external spy service. A dictatorship lends itself to the control of information as power and ensures that it gathers as much information as possible for its policymakers' needs.

The Russians were all about stealing secrets. The United States was its primary opponent, and it would do what it could to obtain U.S. military and political secrets. Our clandestine conflict, or "Cold War," began in the mid-1940s. The leadership under Stalin was greatly concerned about the United States alone having the atomic bomb. Stalin spent great amounts of time and expense using the KGB to target vulnerable Americans, and the USSR succeeded with a nuclear test only four years after that of the United States in the New Mexico desert.

This CI failure launched the FBI and the rest of American intelligence into a spy hunt that lasts to this day. The success rate has been mixed, though the public does tend to hear about the failures. Aldrich Ames, Robert Hanson, and others are the most recent examples of spies who gave away information and damaged the effectiveness of American intelligence to protect its spies in the field, its own agents and even the very means by which they communicated with each other.

Do not think that the issue of CI has gone away in the post 9/11 world. For a while there was an attitude that Al Qaeda was not interested in CI. They obviously were paying attention to our military moves against them and adjusting their tactics accordingly. However, incidents clearly call this attitude into question.

In the years leading to the 9/11 attacks, no single agent of Al Qaeda was more successful in compromising the U.S. intelligence community than Ali Mohamed, a former Egyptian army captain turned CIA operative, Special Forces advisor, and FBI informant. Spying first for the CIA and later the FBI, Mohamed even succeeded in penetrating the John F. Kennedy Special

Warfare Center at Fort Bragg while simultaneously training the cell that exploded a bomb in the World Trade Center in 1993. He went on to train Osama Bin Laden's personal bodyguard, and he photographed the U.S. embassy in Kenya to obtain the surveillance pictures Bin Laden himself used to direct the suicide truck bomb that killed more than 200 people and injured thousands in 1998.[23]

A second, very painful incident reminds us again that our enemy is gaming us in any way possible. In late December 2009, a prominent source on Al Qaeda, recruited by the Jordanian intelligence, turned. At a meeting with CIA officials in Khost, Afghanistan, he committed suicide, taking with him eight people, seven of them CIA officers.[24] While there is an ongoing investigation into the incident, a tape was released that showed him preparing the suicide vest and speaking to the world about his upcoming deed.[25]

In the final analysis, the lessons of compartmentation and CI have been painfully learned and reinforced over the years. The combination of compartmentation issues and CI tend not to create an atmosphere that lends itself to freely sharing information. The challenges of sharing intelligence with members of the law enforcement in the new age of domestic intelligence have been great, and we will address these challenges in detail later in this book.

A BRIEF HISTORY OF DOMESTIC INTELLIGENCE BEFORE 9/11

So now that we have seen the ground rules of the intelligence game, let's look at a brief history of the major players and how domestic intelligence has become a major factor in the American IC.

The U.S. IC is a product of the intelligence failure at Pearl Harbor in 1941 and the immediate rise of the Soviet Union after World War II. From the beginning, it was charged with ensuring there would be no surprises for the United States and to protect us as part of the national security machinery array against the USSR.

The National Security Act of 1947 established the CIA. Headed by the DCI, who reported directly to the president, the CIA was to control all human intelligence collection throughout the world. Its primary target was the USSR. Moreover, it was charged with engaging Moscow throughout the world in support of pro-Western governments. Through covert action (clandestine military or quasi-military support) or through propaganda, the CIA's Plans Directorate was in direct conflict with its Russian counterpart, the KGB.[26]

CIA also had two other parts, a Directorate of Intelligence (DI) and a Directorate of Science and Technology (S&T). The DI published the PDB. This compendium of daily clandestine news contained not only HUMINT but also any other sources of intelligence that might make or inform intelligence to support the president.

The S&T Directorate was focused on methods to support the collection of HUMINT and ways of collecting SIGINT and GEOINT from inside the vast eight million square miles of the USSR. For instance, the S&T developed the first U-2 spy plane and some of the first space reconnaissance satellites.

By 1952, the CIA was joined by the National Security Agency (NSA). Formed to exploit the vast amount of information contained in radio, telegraph, and other signals, NSA surrounded the world with stations to collect information. Located at Fort Meade, Maryland, the "Fort" also was charged with decoding signals and finding and decoding the codes themselves.[27]

NSA has a number of domestic collection successes against "foreign agents," such as Project Venona.[28] While its primary emphasis was collection overseas, the rules under which it operated domestically could be somewhat ambiguous, leading to many accusations in the 1970s of domestic spying. After the Watergate hearings of 1973 and the Church and Pike Committees of 1975–1976 revealed a number of extreme examples, a new law was passed called the Foreign Intelligence Surveillance Act (FISA), which limited these activities to the FBI.[29] The act was created to provide judicial and congressional oversight of the government's covert surveillance activities of foreign entities and individuals in the United States, while maintaining the secrecy needed to protect national security. It allowed surveillance, without court order, within the United States for up to one year unless the "surveillance will acquire the contents of any communication to which a United States person is a party". If a United States person is involved, judicial authorization is required within 72 hours *after* surveillance begins.

The Executive Order 12333, signed by President Ronald Reagan in 1981, further refined restrictions on such domestic activities. Agencies are permitted to collect information that constitutes "foreign intelligence or CI," as long as the agencies do not "acquire information concerning the domestic activities of United States persons."[30]

The other major player during the period before 9/11 was the FBI. While not a part of the IC per se, the FBI has deep relations with the IC and was deeply involved in domestic intelligence collection in the Cold War Era, breaking Soviet diplomatic and intelligence communications codes, which allowed the US and British governments to read Soviet communications. This effort confirmed the existence of Americans working in the United States for Soviet intelligence.[31]

The FBI was also deeply involved in the HUMINT collection of domestic intelligence on Soviet spies, suspected spies, and sympathizers. This effort lasted from the end of the Cold War through the mid-1970s when, like the NSA and CIA, FBI was called to the congressional carpet for its overly zealous efforts. Particularly egregious were the collection efforts against the American civil rights and the Vietnam anti-war movements. Movements were infiltrated by the FBI, and leaders such as Dr. Martin Luther King, Jr., and celebrity supporters such as John Lennon or Jane Fonda were spied upon, taped in their private activities.[32]

THE STATUS QUO FROM 1978–2001

After the tumult of the 1970s, the United States had a system of intelligence that was fixed in place both legally and in the public mind. The CIA and the IC stayed out of domestic intelligence gathering. The FBI did gather domestic intelligence, but only against foreigners or those who interacted with foreign organizations. Sharing of information between the CIA and FBI was strictly regulated. FISA allowed for wiretaps, but use of this technique was strictly regulated through so-called FISA courts, where requests for such taps were made in advance and rarely turned down.[33, 34]

THE WORLD CHANGES, BUT AMERICAN INTELLIGENCE DOES NOT

Nobel Prize winner and astute observer of human nature, George Bernard Shaw once said, "Progress is not possible without change and those who cannot change their minds cannot change anything."

By the mid-1990s, a number of political and technological events were changing the way the world saw itself. International borders were less well defined. The collection of intelligence should have been changing, but it did not.[35]

The last point is a crucial one in advance of the events of 9/11. The end of the Cold War and the fall of the Soviet Union in 1991 precipitated a large cutback in personnel and budget within America's IC. By some public estimates, the cutbacks were in excess of 25 percent of Cold War budgets.[36, 37] This befits the public mood that saw Francis Fukuyama writing about the "end of history" and the Pax Americana.

It also left the U.S. IC bereft of human assets and personnel to deal with a much more complex world with many problems different from those of the Cold War era. As DCI Jim Woolsey said in 1993, "It's as if we were fighting with a dragon for some 45 years and slew the dragon and then found ourselves in a jungle full of a number of poisonous snakes."

There was also a period of time under the Clinton Administration that saw a shift away from the dirty business of HUMINT to the cleaner version of obtaining information through SIGINT. While SIGINT provides excellent intelligence, it does not always allow the analyst to determine motivation, especially among a group of small, tightly involved individuals.

The 1990s saw the rise of the tightly knit terrorist groups whose potential lethality and political prowess earned them the title of "non-nation states," groups with access to weapons and an international reach.

Al Qaeda, with its leader Osama Bin Laden, was the classic case. Devoted to the restoration of an Islamic Caliphate from Europe through Asia and seeing the United States as the leading enemy opposing them, Al Qaeda controlled their membership through the use of small cells and closely guarded communications. They also crossed borders easily, taking advantage of an increasingly complex transportation network around the world and the Internet.

The Internet represents a new and highly unregulated frontier. The Internet is a network of networks that consists of millions of private, public, academic, business, and government networks of local to global scope that are linked by a broad array of electronic and optical networking technologies. It also carries a vast array of information resources and services, most notably the interlinked hypertext documents of the World Wide Web and the infrastructure to support electronic email. The Internet has enabled or accelerated the creation of new forms of human interactions through instant messaging, Internet messaging, Internet forums, and social networking. In addition, no one has any real control over it. These characteristics make the Internet a perfect place for groups like Al Qaeda to hide. It is also very difficult for governments to know where and how to collect information and operate in the Internet.[38]

CONCLUSION

In the final analysis, the intelligence failure of 9/11 was a structural failure. It was less about the way intelligence is gathered or analyzed, or how it is shown to policymakers, and more about the fact that the IC at the time was a system of systems built for another era, a large-scale IC unable to share information either bureaucratically or by law.

It was also about a country that maintained laws better suited for another time. Societies live and die by their shibboleths. We had seen the abuses of the post-Cold War era in domestic intelligence gatherings. Congress, addressing the will of the people, took care of them. In short order, domestic and international intelligence collection was separated. Electronic surveillance was strictly limited. And the FBI, CIA, and other agencies were unable to adapt to the rapidly changing world.

It was also about how the world had changed rapidly in terms of the speed of transportation and information exchange. U.S. policy and its IC failed to grasp this key point. For Al Qaeda and others of its ilk, there are no international borders and no bureaucratic separations. The threat to the United States today is a very different one than we have ever known.

2
Chapter

The Present Threat to America and What We Need to Protect

One of the prime determinants in what kind of intelligence you need is identifying what kind of threat you are facing. This simple concept, however, is often a bone of contention and can become tangled in a process flowing through more political rapids and cross-currents than the normal mind can grasp. And so it has been in post 9/11 America.

Many terms and ideas are thrown around in the threat debate. What is the threat? What is our risk? How can we assess the risk? What does the intelligence say about the threat? How do we manage risk? For now, let's look at this more logically. There is a simple system to break this tangle of ideas apart and define them in a useable and understandable fashion. It is called Risk Management, and it all starts with what you are protecting.

RISK MANAGEMENT—THE CONCEPT

Critical Infrastructure and Key Resources (CIKR)

No country can protect all of its people or all of its infrastructure and resources. A continental nation, like the United States, could spend its entire gross national product and still not cover everything or everyone. So choices need to be made.

The concept of CIKR is a deceptively simple one. You need to choose those resources and infrastructure elements you think are worthy to protect. This is where the simplicity stops and the politics begin.

Ignoring any specific process for the moment, how would you pick the candidates to protect? Do you vote on them? If so, how do you vote? Do you leave the decisions to experts or the politicians themselves? Do you limit these decisions to the national level or leave it to the states and localities to choose?

And what of the comparisons between CIKR's? What is the relative "weight" of protecting a dam versus a nuclear power plant? Are highways more important than schools? Do stadiums out rank office buildings? That, too, is up for debate. The bottom line is that, however you choose CIKR, you have now laid the base for your next step.

The Threat—Where Analysis Enters

The next step is the definition of the threat. Here is where the idea of intelligence enters into the process. What you want from intelligence collection and analysis at this point is the panoply of potential and reasonable threats on the horizon. In other words, who are our enemies and what are their capabilities?

For instance, Al Qaeda is our sworn enemy. Bin Laden and others have issued a fatwa declaring a jihad against us. In their view, it is a Muslim's duty to engage in the struggle against us. Now that you have that one enemy nailed down, what about the others? What about Hezbollah? What about Iran or North Korea? The list of threats can be as long and as varied as you like. There is plenty of information for analysts to look at and plenty of potential threat out there.

Threat Assessment

So, we have now determined which threats are out there. The next step is threat assessment—what can these entities do to their opponents? For instance, a good analyst would examine what means Al Qaeda can bring to bear against us. Do they have nuclear weapons? Are they trying to get access to them? Would they really use them, and how, and against what targets?

A threat assessment also begins the process of separating the chaff from the wheat. As the questions above indicate, it is vital to understand what might be possible for these groups. They may have aspirations, but what can they really pull off? The key to answer that last question is the quality of the data and information you are able to obtain—and, of course, the expertise and insightfulness of your analyst and analytical process.

Risk Assessment

Risk assessment is the culmination of collection and analysis. This is the part of the process where the analyst looks carefully at the threats and the threat assessment and states the likelihood of a threat happening and the extent of damage that it could do if it did take place. From that statement, the decision makers derive a risk assessment determining whether such a thing could happen, how likely it would be, how much damage it could cause, and thus whether it is worth protecting against in relation to other threats.

For example, Al Qaeda detonating a nuclear device at the Port of Long Beach, California, would have devastating effects. But, what is the likelihood of that happening? Analysts would likely agree that is not very probable.

Looking at current trends, Al Qaeda seems to be heading more toward the "lone wolf" attacker. This person would likely wear a suicide belt or build a car bomb to blow up a police headquarters. Easier to do, obviously, than capture or make and detonate a nuclear weapon. You could also do it multiple times at the location of your choice. Yet, the damage a car bomb does would be significantly less than a nuclear weapon. Given the likelihood of the lone wolf, such an attack would likely rank higher than the threat of a nuclear weapon.

You will note that I said such an attack would **likely** rank higher. Once again, this is where politics enter. A good analyst is keenly aware of his audience and should know what their interests are. That does not mean bending the intelligence to suit the audience; however, it does mean that the analyst will know that the suggestion to protect against a less likely but more substantial event (like a nuclear weapon) is clearly going to take a back seat to concerns over the more likely car bombs. That information will clearly affect the decision making of the analyst's audience.

Risk Management—The Final Step

The final step of the process is risk management. This is where the political rubber meets the road. Under the umbrella of risk management you are trying to get the biggest return for your resources and your dollars. How you determine that distribution is a question of influence and politics that reach well beyond any mere analysis.

Here is the risk management equation: Given what we wish to protect, what we know about our enemies' capabilities and desires, and what we think is more likely to happen against that we are protecting, what should we spend on manpower, machinery, and money to protect our designated CIKR? In economics, this type of balancing act is referred to as Pareto optimality. You must seek the maximum utility with the resources you have, trying to please the most people possible, knowing that someone is going to be unhappy.

In a sense, the $40 billion we spend on the DHS is one of the ultimate statements of risk management. We have developed an entire federal organization to coordinate resources and personnel to stop our enemies from harming our CIKR, which also includes the key resource of our citizens.

State and local authorities spend their own funds doing the same thing and seek additional funds from the federal government to manage more risk.

Private companies do the same, using their own funds and matching their own priorities.

One last word on risk management and the role of analysis in it. The traditional IC has always been loath to be "policy prescriptive." In short, they lay out the questions and provide possibilities to better inform the policymaker.[1] The final decision is up to the policymaker.

There is, however, a "new" IC developing that is being asked to go further than the traditional limits and to recommend policy decisions in areas like risk management. These analysts at places like U.S. Immigrations and Customs Enforcement, Transportation Security Administration (TSA), and state and local law enforcement are "closer to the coal face" of "law enforcement policymaking" than their old IC colleagues. They are being made a part of what appears to be a group that embraces a larger and more direct role in the risk management process.

THE FEDERAL GOVERNMENT TRIES

After 9/11, the Bush Administration recognized quickly that some form of risk management process needed to be instituted. But first, they asked the crucial questions: What do we need to protect, how do we select it, and who do we have do it?

On 16 October 2001, according to Executive Order 13286, President Bush established the National Infrastructure Advisory Council (NIAC) to "provide the President . . . with advice on the security of information systems for critical infrastructure supporting other sectors of the economy: banking and finance, transportation, energy, manufacturing, and emergency government services." Executive Order 13286 further states, "The NIAC shall be composed of not more than 30 members appointed by the President. The members of the NIAC shall be selected from the private sector, academia, and state and local government. Members of the NIAC shall have expertise relevant to the functions of the NIAC and generally shall be selected from industry Chief Executive Officers (and equivalently ranked leaders of other organizations) with responsibilities for security of information infrastructure supporting the critical sectors of the economy, including banking and finance, transportation, energy, communications, and emergency government services.[2]

After several iterations and the formation of DHS in 2003, President Bush signed Homeland Security Presidential Directive 7, which ordered the development of a National Infrastructure Protection Plan (NIPP) "to identify and prioritize United States' critical infrastructure and key resources and to protect them from terrorist attacks." The president asked the department to produce the plan in one year, i.e., by December 2004.

This would prove to be no small job. The National Strategy of the Physical Protection of Critical Infrastructures (February 2003) quantified "The Protection Challenge" with the following approximations:

- **Agriculture and Food:** 1,912,000 farms; 87,000 food-processing plants;
- **Water:** 1,800 federal reservoirs; 1,600 municipal waste water facilities;
- **Public Health:** 5,800 registered hospitals;
- **Emergency Services:** 87,000 U.S. localities;
- **Defense Industrial Base:** 250,000 firms in 215 distinct industries;
- **Telecommunications:** 2 billion miles of cable;
- **Energy:**
  - *Electricity:* 2,800 power plants;
  - *Nuclear Power Plants*
  - *Oil and Natural Gas:* 300,000 producing sites;
- **Transportation:**
  - *Aviation:* 5,000 public airports;
  - *Passenger Rail and Railroads:* 120,000 miles of major railroads;
  - *Highways, Trucking, and Busing:* 590,000 highway bridges;
  - *Pipelines:* 2 million miles of pipelines;
  - *Maritime:* 300 inland/costal ports;
  - *Mass Transit:* 500 major urban public transit operators;
- **Banking and Finance:** 26,600 FDIC insured institutions;
- **Chemical Industry and Hazardous Materials:** 66,000 chemical plants;
- **Postal and Shipping:** 137 million delivery sites
- **Key Assets:**
  - *National Monuments and Icons:* 5,800 historic buildings;
  - *Nuclear Power Plants:* 104 commercial nuclear power plants;
  - *Dams:* 80,000 dams;
  - *Government Facilities:* 3,000 government owned/operated facilities;
  - *Commercial Assets:* 460 skyscrapers.[3]

Management of the plan fell to Robert Liscouski, assistant secretary for infrastructure protection at the Information Analysis and Infrastructure Protection (IAIP) Directorate (of DHS). Liscouski told attendees of a conference in October 2004,

> The challenge we have, of course, is that this is not a federal problem but a national problem. And by 'problem' we mean that 85 percent of critical infrastructure assets owned and operated by the private sector require coordination between the federal entities that have responsibility in those sectors, as well as state and local and tribal entities and, of course, the private sector themselves, to

determine exactly what has to be protected and how it has to be protected.[4]

Homeland Security Presidential Directive 7 used the terms "critical infrastructure" and "key resources," referring readers to their definitions in the U.S. PATRIOT Act (critical infrastructure) and the Homeland Security Act of 2002 (key resources):

- **Critical infrastructure**: Systems and assets, whether physical or virtual, so vital to the United States that the incapacity or destruction of such systems and assets would have a debilitating impact on security, national economic security, national public health or safety, or any combination of those matters.
- **Key resources**: Publicly or privately controlled resources essential to the minimal operations of the economy and government.[5]

In February 2005, after the resignation of DHS Secretary Tom Ridge, the DHS released its 50-page Interim National Infrastructure Protection Plan as "a starting point for developing the national, cross-sector plan for critical infrastructure and key resources protection." In this report, the now familiar "CI/KR," or "critical infrastructure/key resources" terminology, was used:

> Protecting our nation's critical infrastructure and key resources (CI/KR) is vital to our national security, economic vitality, and way of life. Attacks on critical infrastructure could disrupt the direct functioning of key business and government activities, facilities, and systems, as well as have cascading effects throughout the Nation's economy and society. Furthermore, direct attacks on individual key assets could result not only in large-scale human casualties and property destruction, but also in profound damage to national prestige, morale, and confidence.[6]

FINALLY A PLAN

On 30 June 2006, DHS announced its first NIPP. It has since been updated twice, with a 2008 interim report and then another version finished in 2009.

In the 2009 version, the overarching goal of the NIPP remains to build a safer, more secure, and more resilient America by preventing, deterring, neutralizing, or mitigating the effects of deliberate efforts by terrorists to destroy, incapacitate, or exploit elements of our nation's CIKR and to strengthen national preparedness, timely response, and rapid recovery of CIKR in the event of an attack, natural disaster, or other emergency.

The 2009 NIPP reflects changes and updates to program elements and concepts laid out in the 2006 plan. It captures the evolution and maturation of the processes and programs first outlined in 2006 without changing the underlying policies. The revised NIPP integrates the concepts of resiliency and protection and broadens the focus of NIPP-related programs and activities to an all-hazards environment.[7]

The Plan also tries to deal with the vast percentage of CIKR that is held in private hands, estimated at more than 80 percent of the CIKR.[8] The Sector-Specific Plans (SSPs) detail the application of the NIPP risk management framework to the unique characteristics and risk landscape of each sector and provide the means by which the NIPP is implemented across all CIKR sectors. Each Sector-Specific Agency developed an SSP through a coordinated effort involving their public and private sector CIKR partners.[9] The NIPP relies on the sector partnership model as the primary organizational structure for coordinating the nation's CIKR protection mission. For each CIKR sector, a Sector Coordinating Council representing the private sector and a Government Coordinating Council have been created to share data, techniques, and best practices, and to support systematic risk-based planning. DHS provides guidance, tools, and support to assist these sector-specific groups in working together to carry out their responsibilities.[10] Those groups include: Agriculture and Food, Banking and Finance, Communications, Defense Industrial Base, Energy, Information Technology, National Monuments and Icons, Transportation Systems, and Water.

The private sector is also making its own plans based on industry groups it has established. The mission of the Information Sharing and Analysis Centers (ISAC) Council is to advance the physical and cyber security of the critical infrastructures of North America by establishing and maintaining a framework for valuable interaction between and among the ISACs and with government.[11] The ISACs, however, are more widely varied than the government plan. They include an Education ISAC, a Public ISAC, a Supply Chain ISAC, and a Multi-State ISAC.

Topping off the large number of participants in American infrastructure protection challenge, state, local, and tribal authorities are trying to address their own problems. By some estimates, there are 17,600 state, local, and tribal protective authorities in the United States.[12] They appear to be left somewhat on their own.

According to the 2009 NIPP, state, local, tribal, and territorial governments are responsible for implementing the homeland security mission, protecting public safety and welfare, and ensuring the provision of essential services to communities and industries within their jurisdictions. They also play a very important and direct role in enabling CIKR protection and resilience, including CIKR under their control as well as that owned and operated by other NIPP partners within their jurisdictions.

WHAT IS THE THREAT AND HOW IS IT DETERMINED?

Now we know what we want to protect. The next step is to identify the threat. As we discussed earlier, if America wants to mitigate the risk of future terror attacks, Washington must first make an accurate assessment of the threat that such events pose and the likelihood of them occurring in the first place.

In an age of globalization, security threats are no longer confined to borders or traditional armies. The Internet, massive immigration flows, and the increasing prevalence of global networks make it much more difficult for policymakers to identify and counteract forces that intend to destabilize the status quo.

In an effort to focus the resources and efforts of the U.S. IC, the DNI sets out each year a presentation to the Congress entitled, "Annual Threat Assessment of the United States Intelligence Community."[13] The document is a list of concerns that the IC believes reflect the current threat level and where its efforts at collection and analysis will be directed that year. Obviously, these threats, composed of input from all 16 members of the IC, are a function of their time and place and often reflect the political concerns of the current day.

In 2010, however, the annual report took on a new tenor that reflected an increased concern on transnational issues that clearly crossed our borders. The leading threat was identified for the first time as Cyber Threat.

According to DNI Admiral Dennis Blair, "The national security of the United States, our economic prosperity, and the daily functioning of our government are dependent on a dynamic public and private information infrastructure, which includes telecommunications, computer networks and systems, and the information residing within. This critical infrastructure is severely threatened."

Blair went to say:

> We face nation states, terrorist networks, organized criminal groups, individuals, and other cyber actors with varying combinations of access, technical sophistication and intent. Many have the capabilities to target elements of the U.S. information infrastructure for intelligence collection, intellectual property theft, or disruption. Terrorist groups and their sympathizers have expressed interest in using cyber means to target the United States and its citizens. Criminal elements continue to show growing sophistication in their technical capability

and targeting. Today, cyber criminals operate a pervasive, mature on-line service economy in illicit cyber capabilities and services, which are available to anyone willing to pay. Globally, widespread cyber-facilitated bank and credit card fraud has serious implications for economic and financial and the national security, intelligence, and law enforcement communities charged with protecting them.[14]

In his presentation, Blair also commented extensively and rather candidly on the threat of terrorism at home and abroad. While acknowledging the continued impact on terrorism abroad by the American military, the DNI noted with concern the rise of outside terrorism coming to America and home-grown terrorism.

In particular, Blair noted that Al Qaeda's "targets that have been the focus of more than one Al Qaeda plot include aviation, financial institutions in New York City, and government targets in Washington, D.C. Other targets Al Qaeda has considered include the Metro system in Washington D.C., bridges, gas infrastructure, reservoirs, residential complexes, and public venues for large gatherings."

The DNI continued, "we cannot rule out that Al Qaeda's interest in damaging the U.S. economy might lead the group to opt for more modest, even "low-tech," but still high-impact, attacks affecting key economic sectors."[15]

After that sobering assessment, Blair then tackled the issue of the growing terrorist threat in America. In a rarity for a DNI, he commented on issues inside the United States, saying,

> Over the past year we have seen ongoing efforts by a small number of American Muslims to engage in extremist activities at home and abroad. The motivations for such individuals are complex and driven by a combination of personal circumstances and external factors, such as grievance over foreign policy, negatively inspirational ideologues, feelings of alienation, ties to a global pan-Islamic identity, and the availability of poisonous extremist propaganda through the Internet and other mass media channels.
>
> We are concerned that the influence of inspirational figures such as Anwar al-Aulaqi will increasingly motivate individuals toward violent extremism. Of particular concern are individuals who travel abroad for training and return to attack the Homeland. Thus far, however, U.S. Intelligence Community and law enforcement agencies with a domestic mandate assess that violence from homegrown jihadists probably will persist, but will be sporadic. A handful of individuals and small, discrete cells will seek to mount attacks each year, with only a small portion of that activity materializing into violence against the Homeland.

The tragic violence at Fort Hood last year underscores our concerns about the damage that even an individual or a small number of homegrown extremists can do if they have the will and access. It is clear, however, that a sophisticated, organized threat from radicalized individuals and groups in the United States comparable to traditional homegrown threats in other countries has not emerged. Indeed, the elements most conducive to the development of an entrenched terrorist presence—leadership, a secure operating environment, trained operatives, and a well-developed support base—have been lacking to date in the United States or, where they have been nascent, have been interrupted by law enforcement authorities . . . a linkage to overseas terrorist groups is probably necessary to transform this threat into a level associated with traditional terrorist groups. We are watching to see how terrorists overseas may try to stimulate such activity.[16]

DNI Blair's assessment for the year was considered sobering and blunt.[17]

THE THREATS IN DETAIL

Terrorism is so threatening precisely because it knows no boundaries; it can take root in weak states such as Somalia, Yemen, and Afghanistan, but also on the vast expanse of the Internet, inside the private and traditional domains of radical mosques, and in the secretive homes of many in Hamburg, London, and New York City. Never before has America attempted to tackle such a nebulous and elusive threat. The fact that the United States is now engaged in two costly wars in Muslim countries indicates the extent to which Washington is trying to deal with the dangers of terrorism. Yet the nature of the threat that terrorism poses is not one that merits the traditional response that any security threat poses, that is, of waging war, going directly to the enemy's front lines, and aiming for total victory. An examination of the qualities of terrorism and other such risks to nation-states in an age of globalization illustrates the need to diversify national responses and counterstrategies.

Many of the most illustrious cases of terrorism's dangers and complexities lie in recent terror attacks or foiled attacks on American soil. The tragic events of 11 September 2001 were perpetrated by 19 men of different nationalities who trained in Afghanistan, planned in Hamburg, and studied in Florida. While their movement was monitored and sometimes flagged as suspicious, not many in Washington could have predicted a highly coordinated attack using four airplanes as guided missiles for separate targets. 9/11 served as wake-up call that, despite the unrivaled status of America as a world superpower, the most dangerous threats can come from the most unexpected places and the weakest states. In an age of globalization, individuals have the capacity to threaten hegemony.

Because terrorists have access to the Internet, they have a chance to spread their message to everyone and anyone with a computer. This accounts for the many non-Middle Eastern subscribers to Al Qaeda's message as well as the increasing prevalence of Al Qaeda offshoots in different regions of the world. Richard Reid, a British citizen with Jamaican ancestry, developed radical views while attending a mosque in Brixton after his numerous prison stints. Reid went on to become the infamous "shoe bomber" who attempted to blow up a U.S. airliner headed for Miami a mere three months after 9/11. Few would have suspected that a petty criminal in South London could possess the capability to inflict massive casualties in accordance with Al Qaeda doctrine. Reid later professed his admiration for Osama Bin Laden, whom he came to follow under the guidance of cleric Abu Hamza al-Mazri at the Brixton Mosque. His case is one of many reminders that the ideology of terror knows no borders or nationalities.

Modern terrorists can cause even more considerable damage than using planes as guided missiles. Globalization and the proliferation of illicit networks in ungoverned states worldwide have made it much easier for terrorists to gain access to chemical, biological, radioactive, and nuclear weapons. The threat of terrorist groups obtaining such a weapon and setting it off in a major American city is real and imaginable. Indeed, there was one such attempt less than a year after 9/11. Jose Padilla, a U.S. citizen, was apprehended at Chicago's O'Hare airport in May 2002 after having returned from Pakistan with the intention of setting off an explosive laced with radioactive material in an attack against America. Padilla was one among many who have tried to use WMDs against the United States. Dhiren Barot, an Indian who grew up in the United Kingdom, was arrested in July 2004 for planning terrorist attacks in New York, Washington, and Newark that involved dirty bombs.[18] Barot's imagined "memorable black day of terror" was never allowed to materialize, in large part thanks to the interrogation and intelligence gathering from captive Khalid Sheikh Mohammed, the principal architect of the 9/11 attacks.

Major American cities are not the only areas of the country under the threat of a major attack. In August 2005, police and federal agents uncovered a terrorist plot by what were initially thought to be bank robbers in Los Angeles. The robbers were actually terrorists. The criminals were discovered to have been planning to use the funds from the robberies to finance terrorist attacks against Los Angeles National Guard facilities, synagogues, and other targets across the Orange County area. In December of that year, the FBI arrested Michael C. Reynolds, an American by birth, for his involvement in a plot to blow up a Wyoming natural gas refinery; the Transcontinental Pipeline, which stretches from the Gulf Coast to New York; and a New Jersey Standard Oil refinery.[19] All of these attacks would have been devastating for

American national infrastructure. Other centers of national power or economic infrastructure have also been targeted, such as the New York Stock Exchange, the Sears Tower, the World Bank, and the Brooklyn Bridge.

The casualties of such attacks would likely dwarf that of 9/11 and be much larger in scale and impact. Terrorists have the will and the capability to strike anywhere on American territory, from coast to coast. While Washington and the hype surrounding the issue of terror may focus on major city centers like New York, the next generation of terrorists is focused on catching us with our eyes closed by striking in less obvious places. Richard Posner has stated, "if Bin Laden is smart he'll attack Des Moines because . . . it's unprotected."

Even more alarming is the fact that there have been terrorists planning right under Washington's nose. In June 2003, the FBI arrested eleven men in Alexandria, Virginia, for weapons counts, violations of the Neutrality Act, and conspiring to support terrorist organizations.[20] Eventually dubbed the "Virginia Jihad Network," the men were found to have contacts with not only Al Qaeda but also the Taliban and Lashkar-e-Taiba, three separate terror groups, each commanding extensive degrees of power. Hailing from a wide variety of backgrounds, including South Korea, Pakistan, and America (including one ex-Marine), the group trained for jihad by participating in paintball tournaments to prepare them for war against the United States.[21] One of the men, Ali Asad Chandia, was a third-grade schoolteacher in College Park, Maryland, which led many in and out of the courtroom to think twice before making a conviction.[22] Federal prosecutor David Laufman stated that Chandia "portrays himself as a mild-mannered, kind individual," but his actual character was uncovered when FBI agents found recordings of him glorifying terrorism, even asking God to "grant safety to Osama Bin Laden." Chandia's involvement in the cell earned him fifteen years in prison, but the central fact remains: terrorists can plan, train, and potentially execute in a wide variety of places and under a wide variety of guises.

Even people who are groomed by the American system for long periods of time can become recruits to the anti-American jihadist cause. On the surface, Aafia Siddiqui's life in America would not have indicated any national security threat. The daughter of middle-class Pakistani parents, Siddiqui's impressive grades as a teenager gained her entrance in the Massachusetts Institute of Technology and Brandeis University, where she graduated in cognitive neuroscience.[23] Yet her ardent Muslim activism and disenchantment with America led her back to Pakistan to marry into Khalid Sheikh Mohammed's family. Less than a year later, U.S. Attorney General John Ashcroft declared Siddiqui one of the seven most-wanted Al Qaeda operatives. America's open borders and lax citizenry qualifications do not serve as a moral deterrent for terrorists.

In fact, quite the opposite seems to be happening, where terrorists are taking advantage of American values in order to plot ever-grander attacks against the country.

The more puzzling aspect of the current threat is nationals who are not from the traditional homelands of terror have committed some of the recent terror attempts. Umar Farouk Abdul Mutallab, the 2009 Christmas Day underpants bomber who tried to ignite an explosive after his plane landed in Detroit, was Nigerian rather than Saudi or Pakistani. If anyone could be called a poster child of globalization as it relates to terrorism, it is Abdul Mutallab: He was raised in Nigeria, Togo, and Kenya, was college-educated in Britain and Dubai, studied Arabic in Yemen, and boarded a plane bound for Detroit in Amsterdam. It is also worth noting that Abdul Mutallab's father is one of the richest men in Africa and is a prominent Nigerian economist. This shatters the traditional notion that terrorists tend to come from underprivileged backgrounds and are simply drawn to terror out of a lack of opportunity. Instead, Abdul Mutallab was well educated, well traveled, and had plenty of career paths available to him. The terrorist threat does not come solely from the poor and desperate; in an era of the Internet and the widespread availability of ideas, anyone can become attracted to the ideology of terror. Furthermore, Abdul Mutallab attempted to carry out the attack in the name of Al Qaeda in the Arabian Peninsula, an offshoot of the original terror group that has gained prominence in recent years. Jihad is a franchise, complete with instructions on how to carry out attacks and start other affiliates and partners. For this reason, radicalization is not something that occurs only outside of American borders.

Indeed, radicalization can happen not only within American borders but also even within American institutions. This is most evidenced by the case of Major Nidal Malik Hasan, the U.S. Army official who went on a shooting spree at the army base in Fort Hood, Texas. Major Hasan was born and raised in Virginia, the son of Palestinian immigrants. His rampage killed 13 fellow soldiers and injured 28 more.[24] It is significant that Hasan was raised in the United States and worked in the American military apparatus, as this should tell Washington that significant threats materialize not only abroad in weak and failed states but also right here at home.

The underlying commonality between both Hasan and Abdul Mutallab is their radicalization by way of communicating online with the radical Yemeni-American cleric, Anwar al-Aulaqi. Al-Aulaqi is purportedly one of the most senior officials behind Al Qaeda in the Arabian Peninsula and is said to have been one of the major reasons behind the offshoot's growth in recent years. The cleric is another prime example of globalization's discontents; born and raised in America and then later in Yemen, the son of a highly prominent Yemeni family, and educated in Colorado, California, and

Washington, D.C., al-Aulaqi has proven adept at recruiting non-Arabic speakers to the jihadist cause due to his charisma and fluency in English.

Al-Aulaqi's influence does not end with Abdul Mutallab and Major Hasan; indeed, FBI officials can trace nearly a dozen American converts to the jihadist cause to the imam. Michael Finton, an American convert to Islam, tried to blow up federal and congressional buildings in Springfield, Illinois, and admired al-Aulaqi's teachings so much that he would quote him on his social networking page. Finton was indicted by a federal grand jury with the charge of attempting to use a WMD against property owned and used by the United States.

Sharif Mobley, an American citizen who was raised a Muslim in New Jersey, left home to live in Yemen to seek out al-Aulaqi as his Al Qaeda mentor. The most disturbing part of Mobley's radicalization was the fact that he worked at five nuclear power plants throughout the United States prior to his departure. That all of these jihadists were drawn to al-Aulaqi's teachings demonstrates the reach of radical Islam in the age of the Internet. Al-Aulaqi now poses such a threat to Americans that the Obama administration authorized his targeted killing in April 2010, an unprecedented presidential action in that it targets an American citizen.[25]

Given the scope of the risks posed by terrorism, it is essential to put it into perspective. Risk management involves an implicit acceptance that risks will never be completely mitigated, as they are inherent in any national or financial undertaking. This means that it is simply impossible for America to prevent every single attack from happening. As evidenced by Abdul Mutallab and Major Hasan, some terrorists will simply slip through the cracks, no matter how many safeguards we erect. While politicians may conveniently blame the IC for "failing to connect the dots," the truth is that there are too many dots on too many different planes to make perfectly accurate assessments. Instead, intelligence analysis is much more like "working on many puzzles—perhaps hundreds of puzzles—simultaneously, and then deciding which puzzle and which piece of that puzzle should take precedence."[26] Therefore, we must come to accept the fact that sometimes, no matter the intensity of our efforts and expenditures, risks will explode without our prior knowledge and despite our intelligence system.

With this in mind, it is important to note that terrorism is not a cause for national alarm and emergency. The threat should not provoke such alarmist tendencies that exaggerate the threat beyond what it actually is. Americans have had the impulse to be inherently reactionary to the slightest hint of a terror attack, quite possibly for good reason given the degree to which the 9/11 attacks shook the national consciousness.

However, panic is not an effective tool for fighting terror. After Abdul Mutallab's botched attempt in December 2009, there were two terror scares in America that in effect proved to be nothing but reactionary hype. Newark Liberty International Airport shut down for hours after a man accidentally walked through the wrong gate.[27] The Meadows Field Airport in California followed the example and closed their own operations down after officials thought they found a "potentially explosive substance" in a traveler's luggage. The substance turned out to be honey, and the hype turned out to be impulsive and counterproductive. If Al Qaeda's aim for the Christmas Day bombing attempt was to throw the American system into chaos, then the group succeeded despite the fact that not a single person was killed.

The fundamental flaw of our approach to terror derives from this alarmist reactionism. After 9/11, Washington responded by implementing one of the largest reorganizations of the federal intelligence bureaucracy in U.S. history, creating the DNI and the National Counter-terrorism Center. Americans have Richard Reid to thank for the fact that U.S. airports now require boarding passengers to take their shoes off prior to entering departure gates. After the Christmas Day bombing scare, not only did two other American airports shut down operations after misidentified threats, but President Obama also planned to utilize costly full-body scanners in a number of airports across the country. These reactions are in themselves a threat to America, because one of the underlying purposes of terror is to provoke a frenzied overreaction—if we are not terrorized, then the attack didn't work.[28] When terrorist networks see the effect that even botched attempts have on American society, they gain and we lose.

This means that Washington must put more emphasis on prevention and preparation than on response when dealing with the terror threat. Having a more robust system that stops terror from happening, coupled with a culture of national preparedness in the event that terror will occur, would do much more to combat the threat than simply reacting with more large-scale expenditures and hype.

Yet it is also necessary to put the threat into perspective. Many have suggested that Al Qaeda's growing weakness is indicated by the desperation of their schemes today when compared to those of 9/11.[29] Whereas on 9/11 the group carried out a highly complex, coordinated, and extensively planned operation using nineteen men and four planes, on Christmas Day an Al Qaeda affiliate launched an operation consisting of one man, no specific target, with an explosive device in his underpants. The fact that the operation was foiled not by intelligence officials but by passengers aboard the plane may also encourage some to speculate that the terror threat is indeed receding: if passengers can stop terrorists in their tracks, then what threat do they really pose? Others may suggest that the terror threat is grossly over-exaggerated.

Paul Campos has said that "a little intelligence and a few drops of courage remind us that life is full of risk, and that of all the risks we confront in

America every day, terrorism is a very minor one." Campos likes to think that the danger of a terror threat occurring on American soil is akin to the dangers of getting murdered or being the victim of a road traffic accident in the United States. Yet these similarities are not accurate, as modern terrorists have the potential to inflict casualties on a massive scale. The more than twenty foiled terror attempts since 9/11 should serve as a reminder that the threat is real and that, if dismissed to be a minor danger, the consequences can be disastrous.

There is the tendency of the American Left to dismiss the threat posed by terrorists today, assuming that Guantanamo detainees and other criminals caught in the War on Terror are simply "sheep herders, dirt farmers, and falcon salesman accidentally swept up on the battlefield."[30] This is simply not true: Between July 2004 and March 2005, tribunals were held for all 558 detainees at Guantanamo. Of these, 520 detainees were found to be enemy combatants, whereas 38 were determined to be non-enemy combatants.[31] This means that the majority of the detainees held at Guantanamo are dangerous terrorists committed to killing Americans.

Marc Thiessen illustrates the risks posed by suspects caught in the War on Terror:

Those detained in Guantanamo include terrorist trainers, bomb makers, recruiters, would-be suicide bombers, and terrorist financiers. More than a dozen were captured with between $1,000 and $10,000 in their pockets, four had between $10,000 and $25,000 on their person, and two more had $40,000 each when apprehended. More than twenty-five have been identified by other detainees as facilitators who provided money, false documents, travel, and safe houses to terrorist operatives. More than thirty-five have been identified as Bin Laden's body guards, and one as Bin Laden's "spiritual advisor."[32]

In other words, many terrorists today are not common criminals, but rather determined mass murderers. This is evidenced by the fact that, when released, many Guantanamo detainees return to the battlefields of Iraq and Afghanistan, where they can continue the targeted killing of American soldiers.

We must make no mistake: Terror does not come from one or two groups, but rather from a wide array of non-state actors and illicit networks. With the Internet, mass telecommunication, and increasing international mobility, these networks have the potential to cause massive civilian damage to America. The terror threat is not receding; instead, it is simply decentralizing.

Today, anyone with access to the Internet can become enchanted by the ideology of radical Islam. In effect, Al Qaeda and other terror groups have "transformed from a central hierarchy to more of a communications hub that exhorts jihadist cells and Islamist lone wolves to commit acts of terrorism and resistance on their own initiative without central direction from the organization."[33] Because the Internet is a vacuum of information for anyone with a cause, the ideology caters not only to the dispossessed and downtrodden but also to those with financial mobility and educated backgrounds. Indeed, this accounts for the number of American recruits to the jihadist cause in recent years. Some, like Jewish-born Adam Gadahn, have been so enchanted by the ideology that they now serve as Al Qaeda senior operatives. Others, such as Colleen LaRose (who dubbed herself "Jihad Jane") seem to simply have caught on via the Internet and taken online sermons to heart.

All in all, this shatters the notion that one can spot a terrorist on appearance. Security officials can no longer limit their watch lists to Arabs that land and depart in U.S. airports or South Asians that wear traditional Islamic garb in major American cities. Racial profiling is not an effective tool because the terror threat is not centralized anymore. The decentralization of jihad compounds the threat of terrorism, making it that much more elusive. The growing attraction of Americans to the cause makes this development clearer than any other. As of April 2010, more than thirty American citizens have been charged with terrorist-related acts.[34]

In an era of globalization, borders no longer serve as deterrents against national security threats. As the forces that propel globalization grow and borders continue to lose significance in the decades to come, illicit networks and non-state actors will find more innovative ways to attract recruits to their cause and carry out more complex and undercover attacks. The terror threat is thus going to continue to become more complicated and diverse.

All of this means that Washington must develop more innovative ways to prevent terror and protect the country in the event of another terror attack. This is central to the concept of risk management; finding the means to mitigate a hazard from occurring and preparing in the event that such a hazard materializes. Terror is one of many risks that every modern nation faces. It is not impossible to strengthen our management of and protection from terror. We just need to accept the fact that it exists, and then develop effective mitigation mechanisms.

3
Chapter

A History of American Spying Abroad and at Home

So we know there is a threat. We have the means to research and anticipate that threat through our intelligence. The question now is how have we dealt with this kind of threat in the past and what lessons can we learn from our experience?

First things first. This is not the first time in its history that America has been threatened from abroad and from within. In the current case, we know who the enemy generally is—primarily Islamic radicals at home and coming in from abroad. We have the means and the understanding to gather information and spy and attempt to track them down. And, like the good American doers we are, we will do what we have to do to get the job done—even if it means cutting corners on a few "rules."

However, Americans also have a certain discomfort with doing the kind of domestic intelligence work that needs to be done to handle this challenge. The spying and the probing and the gathering of information don't sit well with us. These feelings are rooted in our historical and political DNA.

THE AMERICAN PSYCHE

The U.S. Constitution is the psyche of America, and it tells us many things about the American people. Our Founders were children of the 18th-century Enlightenment. They believed in the independence of man and the rights of the person versus the state. They were also pragmatic men, lawyers and businessmen for the most part, who knew you needed a contract to clearly define those rights for the state and the individual. The U.S. Constitution is that contract between the Americans governing and those governed.

The very first article of the Constitution lays out how the people will be represented in this contract. Article One lays out responsibilities of the legislative body, with special note of the two separate but equal houses of the Congress, the Senate and the House of Representatives. The Senate, in its senior advisory role, advises and consents. The House of Representatives is more closely associated with the needs of the people.

Neither legislative branch is hereditary. They are elected at regular intervals: the House every two years, the Senate every six. Both bodies carry the power of the purse over the Executive Branch and may override its objections.[1]

Article Two then outlines the responsibility of the Executive Branch. The Chief Executive will be selected by the people and will be elected every four years. There is a special emphasis on what the President is allowed to do, especially with regard to issues of defense, raising armies, etc. The latter two points are equally addressed in Article One, the power of the legislature, which also has a heavy say in matters of war, namely declaring it and raising money for it.[2]

The place of the Judiciary Branch is outlined in Article Three, where this branch plays the role of overseer. In the final analysis, the Judicial Branch determines whether the rules and actions of the other two branches are "fair."[3]

And, finally, Article Four makes it clear that the states have rights as well, separate from the federal government. While this article has been the bone of contention on a number of civil rights issues over the years, it does clearly provide the states a power of their own to countervail the central government.[4]

So what does this mean for Americans? With three separate and equal branches of government and states' rights, the Constitution says one thing: We don't trust centralized government.

Another rule of the American road is that of honesty and openness. More of a Jeffersonian ideal than his thornier opponent Alexander Hamilton, the good honest American person is our template for behavior. We don't like sneaky people, or people who lie about their lives and intentions. While some might favor Hamilton, it is the Jefferson legend our society lives by.

Given both our Constitution and our Jeffersonian ideals, it is easy to see that spying is somewhat antithetical to American values. The first rule of spying is capturing and securing information clandestinely—the sneaky part. The second rule is to hold that information tightly and give it to few people—primarily only your government. What has "saved it" over the years has been its utility in advancing American interests and its closed world mystique, something that we Americans are drawn to despite our wariness of it. In addition, we have not done it particularly thoroughly or ruthlessly at home against our own people, as have the Russians and the Germans.

This somewhat conflicted American feeling toward spying led to its being on the fringes but not really part of the foreign policy or military sphere in this country for some time. This is not to say that spies have not been there throughout America history. George Washington used spies during the Revolutionary War. Nathan Hale is an example of an intelligence failure well polished.

And, of course, our diplomats overseas effectively acted as our eyes and ears throughout most of the 19th century. The U.S. Navy, too, had its attachés acquiring information. But the material gathered was loosely distributed to the White House and others on a limited and largely unorganized basis.

THE TWENTIETH CENTURY—SPYING BEGINS IN EARNEST

The rise of the imperial system of the late 1800s with England, France, and Germany vying for world power did not leave the United States untouched. Coinciding with the Spanish American War in 1898, American patriotism and its "exceptionalism" began to develop a pretty strong streak of jingoism. We, too, wanted to have a piece of the world. So we took the former Spanish colonies of the Philippines, Puerto Rico, Guam, etc. We sent our White Fleet around the world. We created and built the nation of Panama and the Panama Canal, and we pushed to take our place on the world stage.

We still were reluctant to move forward with any kind of centralized intelligence service. Domestically, things remained as they always had, with a hodgepodge of state and local authorities overseeing any "problems" with aliens. The Department of State and the U.S. Naval attachés overseas, as well as the Navy's Office of Naval Intelligence, provided the War Department and the president with foreign intelligence through various means.

By World War I, America had Naval Intelligence and Army Intelligence gathering both signals and limited human intelligence. Still there was no centralized American spy service such as the British MI-5 and MI-6, or the Russian Cheka, or German military services.[5]

America did take action after several acts of sabotage occurred in the United States. The most famous was the so-called Black Tom incident in 1917, when a large munitions ship in New Jersey was blown up by German saboteurs. The resulting anger, fed by the war fever of the time, caused President Woodrow Wilson along with the Congress to enact some of the harshest laws since the Civil War.

The results were The Espionage Act of 1917 and its later modification, the Sedition Act of 1918. Both acts allowed for local police and federal attorneys to engage in intelligence efforts to prosecute suspected spies.[6, 7] The Espionage Act itself made it a crime:

- To convey information with intent to interfere with the operation or success of the armed forces of the United States or to promote the success of its enemies. This was punishable by death or by imprisonment for not more than 30 years.
- To convey false reports or false statements with intent to interfere with the operation or success of the military or naval forces of the United States or to promote the success of its enemies when the United States is at war, to cause or attempt to cause insubordination, disloyalty, mutiny, refusal of duty, in the military or naval forces of the United States, or to willfully obstruct the recruiting or enlistment service of the United States. This was punishable by a maximum fine of $10,000 fine and up to 20 years in prison.[8]

The Sedition Act forbade the use of "disloyal, profane, scurrilous, or abusive language" about the U.S. government, its flag, or its armed forces or such language that caused others to view the American government or its institutions with contempt. The act also allowed the Postmaster General to refuse to deliver mail that met those same standards for punishable speech or opinion. It applied only to times "when the United States is in war."[9]

The laws themselves came rather late in the war, but prosecutions did take place. By some estimates, approximately fifteen hundred prosecutions were carried out under the Espionage and Sedition Acts, resulting in more than a thousand convictions. It remains unclear what, if any, spying activities the Acts prevented. The laws were repealed after the war in December 1920.[10]

After World War I, the need for domestic and international spying waned a bit. The Palmer Raids of 1919–1920 were attempts by Attorney General A. Mitchell Palmer to arrest and deport left-wing radicals, especially anarchists, from the United States. Based on domestic spying by local police and federal attorneys, some 500 people were deported from the United States. Eventually, the Department of Labor, who executed the deportations, stopped due to qualms about the methods involved and the potential illegalities.[11]

As the events of the late 1930s were leading toward World War II, America tried to do more kinds of intelligence work. The FBI was authorized to follow spies and arrest them in the United States as well as engage in efforts in Latin America. This represented the first real domestic intelligence work done against a foreign enemy in the United States since some limited efforts in and around World War I. And, as always with FBI leader J. Edgar Hoover, it was done in a large-scale way with hundreds of agents focused on enemy aliens and agents of influence like members of the German-American Bund or the pacifist-leaning America First movement.[12]

As in World War I, the State Department collected its own information. The Army and the Navy collected theirs. And no one really shared this information in a centralized way—each having their conduits to the top in their Departments and then on to the President or his staff individually.

The events surrounding 7 December 1941 have been recounted ad nauseum in other books. The lessons drawn here are meant to demonstrate how great an intelligence failure it was, and how it was eventually addressed.

BLAME AND RESOLUTION

There were a number of warnings from both human and signals intelligence that an attack would likely take place on American soil in the Pacific by the Japanese. What did occur took the military by surprise and led to the now predictable series of Congressional investigations. Blame was established, primarily against Commander of the Pacific Fleet, Admiral Husband E. Kimmel.[13]

However, Pearl Harbor was also America's first large-scale intelligence failure. And like most intelligence failures, it did not involve stupid people, but a system that simply was not built to handle a changing threat.

First, there was no real organized system of intelligence collection and analysis within the U.S. government. State Department diplomats passed information back to Washington. There it arrived at individual country desks that passed it to their leadership, who passed it on to select personnel at the White House. The FBI covered the United States and Latin America, collecting human intelligence. Information from the FBI leadership was passed to the Attorney General and select people at the White House. Army and Navy signals intelligence and code decryption was passed to appropriate high levels in both services. They in turn passed it to select people at the White House. There was a lot of information with no central point of collection, and analysis of the information was minimal at best with information passed on but without context.

Even after the investigations following Pearl Harbor, intelligence collection was jealously guarded by individual organizations. The FBI, Army, and Navy never surrendered their intelligence dominance in their areas.

However, in an effort to boost overseas human intelligence collection, the White House (over senior Army and Navy officers objections) established the Office of Strategic Services (OSS) in June 1942, America's first real spy service.

Placed under the nominal control of the Army, the OSS, jokingly referred to as "Oh So Social" for its many upscale, Ivy League officers, was headed by General William "Wild Bill" Donovan. Donovan was a New York lawyer and a friend of President Franklin D. Roosevelt, who had served in the Fighting 69th Division of World War I. Donovan placed the focus of the

OSS on human intelligence and covert support of partisan groups behind enemy lines.

After the successful conclusion of the war in September 1945, the Truman Administration intended to quickly dismantle the OSS, fearing comparisons to the activities of the German Gestapo during the war. However, the aggressive nature of the Soviet Union began to change Truman's mind.

In mid-1945, the OSS's analytical arm, the Research and Analysis Branch, was spun off to the State Department as the still extant INR. By January 1946, Admiral Sidney Souers was appointed by the president to be the first DCI. Souers oversaw a small office that coordinated intelligence in the United States and could support the White House on intelligence matters.[14]

Truman then proposed to his Administration that a centralized intelligence agency be created. The reply was not favorable, with a particularly vehement denunciation from a territorial J. Edgar Hoover at the FBI, who dismissed the idea out of hand.[15]

THE COLD WAR ERA—AND SPYING IN AMERICA

Still, Truman went to the Congress, and in 1947 the National Security Act was passed, setting up the National Security Council, the Air Force, the Joint Chiefs of Staff, and the CIA. In 1948, a combination of National Security Council guidance and a Congressional bill clearly delineated the CIA's activities. They were to include the authority to carry out covert operations "against hostile foreign states or groups or in support of friendly foreign states or groups but which are so planned and conducted that any U.S. government responsibility for them is not evident to unauthorized persons." The guidance also stated that the CIA was going to be responsible for collecting human intelligence overseas and provide analysis for the president. America had its first true spy organization.[16, 17]

The establishment of the CIA gave the president a tool he never had before, one that allowed a civilian organization to take part in paramilitary-like assignments overseas. This kept the U.S. military out of actions that would be seen as provocative. It would also give the president plausible deniability, with the CIA available to take the blame for covert actions by the U.S. government.

All of this was necessary weaponry for the president's use. The creation of the CIA was prompted by a very aggressive Soviet Union, whose own spy service was deeply involved in activities around the world. With emphasis on the overthrow or neutralization of pro-Western governments, the KGB was Russia's secret foreign policy. The KGB supplied lethal aid and training to many communist organizations around the world, such as the Greek communists during the 1946–1948 civil war. Moscow also provided extensive support to left-wing unions in Western Europe, trying influence local elections. They were also doing their best in the United States through a network of agents to steal our atomic secrets and gain insight into our political hierarchy's decision making.

It is in this period, from 1944–1949, during the increasing fears of communist influence at home and abroad that Project Venona was started. Based on the collection of Army and Navy signals intelligence, and in cooperation with the British, decrypted messages gave insights into Soviet behavior in the period.

With the first break into the Soviet spy code, Project Venona revealed the existence of Soviet espionage at Los Alamos National Laboratories. Identities soon emerged of other American spies in service to the Soviet government. The results of the spying showed that the United States and other nations were targeted in major espionage campaigns by the Soviet Union as early as 1942.

Some spies even worked in Washington in the State Department, the Treasury Department, the OSS, and the White House. Among those identified are Julius and Ethel Rosenberg; Alger Hiss; Harry Dexter White, the second-highest official in the Treasury Department; Lauchlin Currie, a personal aide to Franklin Roosevelt; and Maurice Halperin, an OSS section head.[18]

Domestic intelligence efforts were particularly given a boost by the very public Rosenberg spy trial in 1951, in which KGB agents clearly had recruited people associated with our nuclear program. The Rosenberg conviction pushed in earnest the "anti-spy build up" within America to root out such influences.[19]

THE FBI TAKES ITS PLACE

The history of this anti-spy period of the McCarthy era and the House Un-American Activities Committee is not one that covers America with glory. While some communist influence was discovered, many more people were tarred with the brush of being "red" and had their livelihoods and reputations destroyed. While this was focused on a narrow part of the population, the fear spread in general and was the zeitgeist of most politics in the 1950s.

From an operational viewpoint, the collection of information by the FBI, CIA, and Army human intelligence elements within the United States grew relatively unchecked. With J. Edgar Hoover in the lead pressing the hunt, there was remarkable coordination of efforts focusing on influences at home, and the review went from communist agents to "communist sympathizers."

Hoover had been stung in the late 1940s that his FBI (he would be the head until his death in 1972) had not had a more direct hand in the rooting out of spies in America. That approach quickly changed. Hoover eventually ended up receiving the information produced by Project Venona. This allowed the FBI to pursue prosecutions against suspected spies.

Frustrated by a 1956 Supreme Court ruling that favored limits on the Justice Department's ability to prosecute people for their political opinions (most notably, Communist), Hoover decided to engage in a larger scale program that was tightly controlled by the FBI.

COINTELPRO (an acronym for Counter-Intelligence Program) was a series of covert and often illegal projects conducted by the FBI aimed at investigating and disrupting dissident political organizations. According to its own records, the FBI used covert operations from its inception; however, formal COINTELPRO operations took place between 1956 and 1971.[20] The FBI's stated motivation at the time was "protecting national security, preventing violence, and maintaining the existing social and political order."

As the civil rights movement dawned and gained strength in the mid-1950s and early 1960s, Hoover turned his sights on organizations such as the Southern Christian Leadership Conference and its leadership, including Nobel Prize winner Dr. Martin Luther King, Jr. Groups associated with anti-Vietnam War efforts were also targeted. Files were kept on American citizens regardless of whether they engaged in protest or were openly sympathetic to issues Hoover regarded as anti-American. Eventually, even ex-Beatle John Lennon came under scrutiny.[21]

According to FBI records, 85 percent of COINTELPRO resources were expended on infiltrating, disrupting, marginalizing, and/or subverting groups suspected of being subversive, such as communist and socialist organizations; the women's rights movement; black nationalist groups; the non-violent civil rights movement, including individuals such as Dr. Martin Luther King, Jr., and others associated with the Southern Christian Leadership Conference, the National Association for the Advancement of Colored People, the Congress of Racial Equality, the American Indian Movement, and other civil rights groups; a broad range of organizations labeled "New Left," including Students for a Democratic Society, the National Lawyers Guild, the Weathermen, almost all groups protesting the Vietnam War, and even individual student demonstrators with no group affiliation; and nationalist groups such as those "seeking independence for Puerto Rico."[22]

While Hoover and the FBI are most often blamed for overzealousness during this period, they were not alone in this process. Presidents and Attorneys General from the Eisenhower Administration through the Nixon Administration approved wiretaps and enthusiastically accepted information on domestic "enemies," communist or otherwise.[23] The CIA later revealed that it had illegally conducted surveillance on some 7,000 U.S. citizens involved in the anti-war movement. The CIA had also experimented on people, who unknowingly took LSD.[24]

DOMESTIC INTELLIGENCE RESTRICTED

The break in this first U.S. engagement in American internal spying came in 1972. Watergate stands for many corruptions, but one of them carried domestic spying to new levels. The so-called "Plumber's Operation," searching for leakers of information and set up out of the White House, was executed with the direct approval of President Richard Nixon. Involving both former FBI and CIA agents who used past connections in their work, it was originally designed to track intelligence leaks out of the White House.

Originally prompted by the New York Times leak of Pentagon Papers on the conduct of the Vietnam War—specifically leaked to them by Daniel Ellsberg of RAND—the group began to extend its scope to include political enemies. On 17 June 1972, Plumber operatives were caught in the act of checking electronic bugs in the offices of the Democratic National Committee located in the Watergate Building in Washington, D.C.

The subsequent 1973 Watergate hearings in the U.S. Senate and the follow-up hearings on FBI and CIA activities in the United States stopped domestic spying against U.S. citizens in its tracks. Admissions by former and current members of the FBI and CIA confirmed the worst in the minds of the public. Legal and public retribution was at hand.

As with all political scandals, a number of committees and commissions sprung up in the aftermath of the Watergate exposures to review and correct the past mistakes and hash over the ashes. The Senate established the Church Committee. The House established the Pike Committee. And the president, now Gerald Ford, appointed Vice President Nelson Rockefeller to head an Executive Branch commission.

The results were the first real oversight conducted on the IC, including collection efforts focused at home. The U.S. Congress set up select committees in the Senate and House to oversee IC matters of budget and program.[25] The Ford Administration, on the basis of Rockefeller's recommendations, put through Executive Order 11905, which limited U.S. foreign intelligence gathering at home to foreign nationals and U.S. citizens who volunteer information. The CIA was strictly forbidden from spying on U.S. individuals and would have limited contact with the FBI, providing only material that related to foreign nationals on U.S. soil.[26]

The use of the Executive Order by Ford was meant to send a message to both the public and the government that domestic intelligence was henceforth going to be strictly controlled. Executive Orders have been used by presidents since 1789, usually to help officers and agencies of the Executive Branch manage the operations within the federal government itself, and they have the full force of law. This Executive Order was the first to affect the operations of the CIA and FBI.

With the election of President Jimmy Carter in 1976, the new Administration felt it had an even greater mandate to control American intelligence gathering more tightly. While it would engage with Congress on further legal restrictions on domestic intelligence, the Carter Administration conducted a National Security Council review in 1977. They pushed forward another Executive Order.

Carter's Executive Order 12036, executed in January 1978, further tightened oversight with the Executive Branch through Presidential advisory boards and further limited the type of domestic information the FBI could gather.[27]

In October 1978, the last piece was put in place for this new, strict control of domestic intelligence: the Foreign Intelligence Surveillance Act of 1978 (FISA). This act placed tight restrictions over the use of domestic wiretaps by the FBI. FISA did not forbid wiretaps, but it required the FBI to provide a written request to a specially cleared federal judge. The judge would then rule on the merits of the case and grant or decline the wiretap.[28]

Thus, the pieces were set in place. Executive Order 12036, Congressional oversight, and FISA would oversee and prevent any further abuses in the system. Moreover, a more sensitized public was willing to support such groups as the American Federation of Scientists, who gathered information about intelligence efforts and made them available to the public. The times had changed.

With the election of the Reagan Administration in 1980, the assumption was that restrictions on domestic intelligence might be modified. That was not the case. However, the Reagan Administration did issue a new Executive Order, 12333, that allowed some types of assassination efforts overseas but changed nothing about the collection or use of domestic intelligence. And so the oversight stayed in line through 2001.[29]

THE INTELLIGENCE FAILURE OF 2001 AND THE RISE OF DOMESTIC INTELLIGENCE

And so we arrive at old world 11 September 2001. Overall, intelligence budgets have been flat or in decline since the collapse of the Soviet Union; personnel had declined by nearly a quarter.

Domestic intelligence in the United States is confined to the FBI, whose main resources since the fall of the Berlin Wall in 1989 have shifted to white-collar crime. It also continues the time-honored tradition of its field units fighting or ignoring headquarters' operations. CIA and others in the IC have little contact with the FBI except through relatively distinct efforts like the CIA's Counter-Terrorism Center (CTC), which focused on international terrorist organizations. FISA is in place, and Congressional oversight remains, though spotty in its presence and thoroughness.

Other potential areas of domestic security are at best spotty. Thanks to a number of plane hijackings and terrorist incidents overseas, watch lists have been prepared and managed by the CIA and State Department for passage to Customs, Border and Immigration personnel. The databases are disjointed and poorly coordinated. While there had been plans to coordinate hijacking strategies with the military, communications between the Federal Aviation Administration and the U.S. military were limited at best.[30]

Throughout the summer, there had been warnings from various human and signal sources that something big was planned for the fall. On 6 August 2001, a PDB article noted that such an attack was imminent and possibly could take place on the United States. There were, however, no further details. Despite efforts by DCI George Tenet and National Security Council Terrorism Advisor Richard Clarke to share their concerns, little if any preparation was made on the U.S. mainland.[31]

Then came the disaster of 9/11, when, in a little more than 90 minutes, nearly 2,800 American civilians were killed in New York City, Washington, D.C., and Pennsylvania.[32] It is by this event that the world of intelligence was deeply shaken, and the rebirth of domestic intelligence occurred over a relatively short three-year time span.

The Bush Administration moved quickly to plug the most immediate and obvious gaps that led to this failure. In cooperation with Congress, the TSA was established in November 2001 to oversee all airline travel in the United States. The position of a Special Assistant to the President for Homeland Security was established in October 2001, headed by former Pennsylvania governor Tom Ridge, to coordinate duties among agencies in the United States that dealt with "homeland protection" issues.

On 26 October 2001, President Bush signed the Uniting and Strengthening America by Providing Appropriate Tools Required to Intercept and Obstruct Terrorism Act of 2001 (U.S.A. PATRIOT Act).[33] From this foundation document, the U.S. government moved heavily into domestic intelligence. It increased the ability of law enforcement agencies to monitor telephone and e-mail communications as well as medical, financial, and other records. This law eased restrictions on foreign intelligence gathering within the United States; expanded the Treasury's authority to regulate financial transactions, particularly those involving foreign individuals and entities; and broadened the discretion of law enforcement and immigration authorities in detaining and deporting immigrants suspected of terrorism-related acts. The act also expanded the definition of terrorism to include domestic terrorism.

Modifying nearly one hundred years of American domestic policy, the Bush Administration created a United States Northern Command in its armed forces. Created in October 2002, its mission is to protect the United States homeland and support local, state, and federal authorities. The support that the United States Northern Command provides to civil authorities is still limited by the Posse Commitatus Act of 1887 and the Insurrection Act of 1807, which limits the role of the U.S. military in civil law enforcement. To reinforce its strength, the Command's number two would include the highest-ranking member of the National Guard.[34, 35]

It also became clear that the U.S. government needed more than a special assistant to organize homeland security cooperation. In October 2002, Congress passed a bill in which twenty-two formerly separate agencies were combined into the DHS.[36] This massive grouping was unique in U.S. government history and cut quite a swath. Included in the new DHS were such major players as Coast Guard, Customs, Border Guard, Immigration, and Federal Emergency Management. It became our first ever version of a ministry of interior focused on internal protection.

In addition to this gathering of agencies, two senior positions were established in the leadership structure. One Assistant Secretary was to focus on infrastructure protection advising on what in the United States should be protected. Another Assistant Secretary would focus on the kinds of intelligence American leadership needs to make the country safe. This person was also charged with helping state and local "first responders" get the kind of information and analysis they need to protect their local communities.

You will notice that the FBI was not mentioned in this flurry of activities. During the 2001–2003 period, the FBI shifted about a third of its resources to its nascent National Security Division and its counter-terrorism efforts under the U.S.A. PATRIOT Act. It skillfully avoided any inclusion in the new DHS. More additions to the homeland constellation were coming.

The 9/11 Commission, founded in November 2002 and jointly chartered by the president and Congress to review the events of that day, wrote its final report in May 2004. It recommended a coordinating body for all terrorist information reporting to the president. And thus, taking a smaller group created in the wake of 9/11 to do such, the NCTC was born. The NCTC was charged with pulling together all the information databases from around the U.S. government and making an assessment of threats against America on a daily basis—a threat matrix. This matrix would be briefed to the President daily. NCTC was also required to reach out to the state and local communities around the country to provide them information of a timely and useful nature.

THE OLD INTELLIGENCE COMMUNITY IS NO MORE

The DCI issued the Iraq WMD National Intelligence Estimate in October 2002. Briefed to the President and at the United Nations, it was used as a basis for which to go to war with the Saddam Hussein regime in Iraq. All controversies aside, it was dead wrong.

After the 9/11 debacle, the Congress stepped in to attempt a legislative remedy. The Bush Administration created the so-called WMD Commission by executive order in early 2004. First established to review the Iraq WMD mistake, it soon morphed into a committee to recommend changes to the IC.

The Congress, believing the intelligence oversight committees had failed in their duties, assigned the re-creation of the IC to its Government Affairs (Senate) and Government Reform (House) committees. While these committees are responsible for the reformation of the Executive Branch, it was a slap in the face of the House Permanent Select Committee on Intelligence and the Senate Select Committee on Intelligence. This decision also began a mad dash to advise the committees from both the Executive Branch and the intelligence committees.

What resulted from the committees' efforts was the October 2004 Intelligence Reform and Terrorist Prevention Act (IRTPA). This last block of reform was meant to change the National Security Act of 1947 itself. The bill appointed a new DNI. This DNI would oversee programs and budgets for all sixteen intelligence programs in the federal government. This role would be separated from the duties of the CIA to focus exclusively on these relations. The new DNI would also advise on Director appointments for the agencies of the IC. The newly created NCTC would report to the DNI, who also controlled the PDB.

As with all things, the devil is in the details. The Department of Defense, (DOD) under Secretary of Defense Donald Rumsfeld, objected to anyone but the DOD controlling defense intelligence assets. He had even created a new position of Undersecretary of Intelligence to suit his in-house needs. As more than 80 percent of the IC is part of the DOD, the DNI could say little about it.

A closer read of the DNI powers also showed that this role would have little power over budgets or programs and would act primarily in an advisory role. The DNI's main efforts would be funneled in that direction, though the DNI began tackling the sticky issue of information and intelligence analysis sharing outside the IC.

HOW DOES THIS AFFECT ME?

As a citizen of the United States, I am a self-interested partisan. In short, as they say in the political arena, I vote my pocketbook—as do a lot of other people. While the machinations on the national level are interesting, and those on the local level are even more interesting, what does this domestic intelligence stuff mean to me?

The first manifestation of this was the airport check-in line. We were already used to some of this before 9/11. After 9/11, it got much worse. As all 19 hijackers effectively waltzed through the current system of the day, changes need to be made—and made quickly.

After a total shutdown of the system for several days, American planes were once again in the air. The immediate restrictions were relatively harsh. Bags were checked. People were checked. There was no real established procedure around the country, and the lines at airports grew to be hours long.

The bureaucratic answer to airline safety came from Washington. Prior to 9/11, the airlines were responsible for security, often in cooperation with the local airport. The two famous questions were the initial screening: ticket counter agents were required to ask two questions of passengers checking luggage:

- Have any of the items you're traveling with been out of your immediate control since the time you packed them?
- Has anyone unknown to you asked you to carry an item aboard the aircraft?

Visitors had to pass through metal detectors and have their carry-on luggage X-rayed before entering the concourses. Boarding passes and photo ID were not required, as at that time the concourse was still viewed as a public area.

TRANSPORTATION SAFETY

On 19 November 2001, less than two months after 9/11 and in record time for Washington, the TSA was created. The TSA was the first part of the new post 9/11 bureaucracy with whom most Americans would come in contact.

Created as part of the Aviation and Transportation Security Act,[37] TSA was originally part of the Department of Transportation. Eventually, in November 2002, it was moved under DHS. To put it bluntly, TSA was now in charge of all security in all means of transportation. TSA eventually developed a number of approaches to protecting the American transportation system, including:

- Transportation Security Officer, also known as a screener, who performs security screening of persons and property and controls entry and exit points within an airport. They also practice surveillance of several areas beyond the checkpoint and before it in specialized programs implemented by the TSA.
- Federal Air Marshal, a federal law enforcement officer who, while blending in with passengers, is tasked with detecting, deterring, and defeating terrorist or other criminal hostile acts targeting U.S. air

carriers, airports, passengers, crew, and when necessary, other transportation modes within the nation's general transportation systems.

- Transportation Security Inspectors conduct comprehensive inspections, assessments, and investigations of passenger and cargo transportation systems to determine their security posture. TSA employs roughly 1,000 aviation inspectors, 450 cargo inspectors, and 100 surface inspectors.

- The National Explosives Detection Canine Team Program prepares dogs and handlers to serve as mobile teams that can quickly locate and identify dangerous materials that may present a threat to transportation systems. As of June 2008, the TSA had trained about 430 canine teams, with 370 deployed to airports and 56 deployed to mass transit systems.[38]

The next system to directly affect Americans (and Canadians and Mexicans) was tighter border security. Some of the 9/11 hijackers had slipped through the Canadian border into Bangor, Maine. This, too, was something the federal government wanted to stop.

BORDER SECURITY

The Border Patrol was founded in May 1924 as an agency of the United States Department of Labor to prevent illegal entries along the United States–Mexico border and the United States–Canada border. It was not an easy job. The border with Canada covers about 5,500 miles (including Alaska), and the border with Mexico is nearly 2,000 miles long.[39] No part of either border has a permanent military presence, a rarity in the world today.

The agency was founded "at the height of Prohibition in the United States, and organized crime was a growing concern, as the mafia controlled a majority of the alcohol being smuggled into the United States."[40] As a result of the 9/11 attacks and Border Patrol's merging into the DHS in 2005, the Border Patrol's current task is to prevent terrorists and terrorist weapons from entering the United States. However, the Border Patrol's traditional mission remains as the deterrence, detection, and apprehension of illegal immigrants and individuals involved in the illegal drug trade who generally enter the United States in many ways other than through designated ports of entry.

It takes a small army to perform this job. The Border Patrol employs more than 20,200 agents (as of the end of fiscal year 2009), who are specifically responsible for patrolling the 6,000 miles of Mexican and Canadian international land borders and 2,000 miles of coastal waters. The Border Patrol also operates thirty-three permanent interior checkpoints along the southern border of the United States surrounding the Florida Peninsula and the island of Puerto Rico. Agents are assigned primarily to the Mexico–United States border, where they are assigned to control drug trafficking and illegal immigration.[41]

In November 2005, the Border Patrol published an updated national strategy. The goal of this updated strategy is operational control of the United States border. The strategy has five main objectives:

1. Apprehend terrorists and terrorist weapons illegally entering the United States;
2. Deter illegal entries through improved enforcement;
3. Detect, apprehend, and deter smugglers of humans, drugs, and other contraband;
4. Use "smart border" technology; and
5. Reduce crime in border communities, improving quality of life.[42]

With regard to the second and third objectives, there has been much controversy. In 2006, The Secure Fence Act of 2006 was signed into law.[43] The act allows for more than 700 miles of double-reinforced fence to be built along the border with Mexico, across cities and deserts alike, in the U.S. states of California, Arizona, New Mexico, and Texas, areas that have experienced illegal drug trafficking and illegal immigration

The act also authorizes the installation of more lighting, vehicle barriers, and border checkpoints, as well as more advanced equipment like sensors, cameras, satellites and unmanned aerial vehicles in an attempt to watch and control illegal immigration into the United States. Officials say that it will help cut down on the number of illegal vehicles that go back and forth across the border bringing illegal drugs.

The project has been troubled from day one. As of mid-2010, the fence itself is far from complete, with numerous contractual problems encountered by the Border Patrol and with Congressional action pending to see why it has yet to be finished.[44] In addition, immigration groups regard the fence as an assault on those trying to find a better life in America.[45]

OTHER BORDER INITIATIVES

Beyond the fence on the Mexican border, there have been other initiatives that impact border security. As of 2009, American citizens are required to bring their passport or similar identification documents to cross the Canadian and Mexican borders. This means that all persons crossing the border are required to report to the respective customs and immigration agencies in each country.[46]

On 27 March 2008, DHS and the Department of State announced their final outline for the land and sea portion of the Western Hemisphere Travel Initiative (WHTI).

A core 9/11 Commission recommendation (and IRTPA), the WHTI final rule requires travelers to present a passport or other approved secure document denoting citizenship and identity for all land and sea travel into the United States. WHTI establishes document requirements for travelers entering the United States who were previously exempt, including citizens of the United States, Canada, and Bermuda. These document requirements will be effective June 1, 2009."[47]

At the time, then Secretary of Homeland Security Michael Chertoff said, "Limiting and standardizing the types of documents presented will result in a more secure and efficient border. We will continue to encourage cross-border travel and trade while at the same time decreasing identity theft and fraud."

On the latter point, cross-border transportation companies, such as members of the trucking industry, were not happy. They noted that, despite efforts to create frequent-user cards, the border crossings would be particularly backed up, thus affecting their delivery times and their customers. Civil rights advocates expressed concerns over the use of electronic data chips in passports that might speed up the process of crossing the border.[48]

BORDER INTELLIGENCE GATHERING AND DATABASES

As we have reviewed in detail, America has tightened its borders since 9/11, and it has introduced a number of technologies and methods to help in the process. Everything from fences to electronic chips in passports is being tried. Ultimately, the question is this: Whom do you let in, and how do you determine that they are "safe"?

In future chapters, we will discuss the rise of federal, state, and local government databases and some of the concerns around them in terms of access and the type of information contained in them. For the purposes of this chapter, let's take a brief look at a few databases that now exist to assist the border watchers and others surveilling inside the United States.

As a small-town wit noted after the May 2010 Times Square bombing attempt, "Nearly nine years after 9/11, there is still no functional interoperability among an alphabet soup of national security and criminal databases, including NAILS, TECS, CLASS, VISAS, VIPER, TUSCAN, TIPPIX, IBIS,

CIS, APIS, SAVE, IDENT, DACS, AFIS, ENFORCE, and the NCIC."[49] Shane Harris, counter-terrorism reporter for the *National Journal*, put it even more succinctly: We have "80 different streams of information on 28 databases."[50]

The first list most of us encounter is used at the airport, the so-called "No-Fly List." The No-Fly List is a list, created and maintained by the FBI's Terrorist Screening Center, of people who are not permitted to board a commercial aircraft for travel in or out of the United States. The list, which includes 6,000 names, has also been used to divert aircraft not flying to or from the United States away from U.S. airspace.[51]

The No-Fly List—along with the Secondary Security Screening Selection, which tags would-be passengers for extra inspection—was created after the 9/11 attacks. A "false positive" occurs when a passenger who is not on the No-Fly List has a name that matches or is similar to a name on the list. Such a passenger will not be allowed to board a flight unless they can differentiate themselves from the actual person on the list, usually by showing a middle name or date of birth. The most famous example of the false positive was the late Senator Edward Kennedy (D-MA).[52]

The No-Fly List is different from the Terrorist Watch List, also managed by the FBI, which is estimated to exceed one million names of people suspected of some involvement with terrorism.[53] As might be expected, organizations like the American Civil Liberties Union (ACLU) are concerned that the list has gotten out of hand, with an estimated 20,000 names being added every month.[54]

Another example of this individual encounter with government is occurring at the state and local level and is being done much more quietly. A *Washington Post* story from April 2008, based on an unidentified leaked document, reported that "intelligence centers (fusion centers) run by states across the country have access to personal information about millions of Americans, including unlisted cell phone numbers, insurance claims, driver's license photographs, and credit reports."[55]

Most of the centers have subscriptions to Accurint, ChoicePoint's Autotrack, or LexisNexis. These information brokers are Web-based services that deliver instant access to billions of records on individuals' homes, cars, phone numbers, and other information. Some of the centers link to records of currency transactions and almost 5 million suspicious-activity reports filed by financial institutions with the Treasury Department's Financial Crimes Enforcement Network. One center also has access to top-secret data systems at the CIA, the document shows, though it's not clear what information those systems contain.[56]

Government watchdogs, along with some police and intelligence officials, said they worry that the fusion centers do not have enough oversight and are not transparent enough for the public, in part because they operate under various state rules. The *Washington Post* article quotes Jim Dempsey, vice president for public policy at the Center for Democracy and Technology, a nonpartisan watchdog group: "Fusion centers have grown, really, off the radar screen of public accountability. Congress and the state legislatures need to get a handle over what is going on at all these fusion centers."[57]

So why is this collection of information about American persons of such concern to them? In the next chapter, we will discuss how this type of government activity has penetrated the American psyche.

4

Chapter

Why American Intelligence Is So Challenging

America is a world power and a continental power. Our political and military commitments span the globe. We have a nation of fifty states covering nearly 4 million square miles—the third largest country in the world. We are extravagantly subdivided into tens of thousands of small political and economic districts. To say the least, America is a diffuse country with diffuse interests. Its IC is a reflection of that diffuseness. Like all bureaucracies, it is also a function of its own organization and its own hard-to-break rules.

As we have discussed, America's IC has grown from one agency to sixteen in less than sixty years. The CIA was established first in 1947 by President Truman to coordinate the "nation's intelligence activities and correlate, evaluate, and disseminate intelligence affecting national security."[1] At that time, the CIA was the sole and principal intelligence arm of the U.S. government.

Today, that responsibility is shared by Air Force Intelligence, Army Intelligence, the CIA, Coast Guard Intelligence, the DIA, the Department of Energy, the DHS, the Department of State, the Department of Treasury, the DEA, the FBI, Marine Corps Intelligence, the National Geospatial-Intelligence Agency, the National Reconnaissance Office, the NSA, Navy Intelligence, and the new Office of the DNI (Figure 4.1 here—Current U.S. Intelligence Community).[2]

The growth of the IC has not been a particularly regulated one. The DCI was to have nominal control over its activities, but the vast majority of resources among these other parties are controlled by their "home" department or bureau. The DNI was established in 2004 to remedy that problem; however, it has had little impact so far, as we will discuss later in the book.

So, the IC is less a community than it is an agglomeration of interests. Or, as the joke goes, it is neither intelligently set up or much of a community. So

Figure 4.1

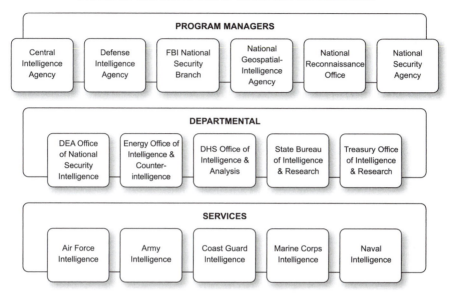

why the proliferation of spy agencies? The first reason is the simplest one: No one has ever wanted a comprehensive U.S. intelligence service. From the earliest times on, as we have discussed, there has been a fear of a centralized spy service like the German Gestapo or the Russian KGB, covering both internal and external spying activities.

The second reason is a more political one. From the beginning, each part of the federal government involved in intelligence wanted their own people. Not a bad motivation because each organization has a different purpose, and the one-size-fits-all approach would not likely work.

For instance, the State Department needs an intelligence service to provide analysis in tune with its detailed political maneuvers overseas. Thus, the INR interacts closely with the State Department desks overseeing diplomatic efforts in different countries and on transnational issues, both providing analysis and using the insights of State Department diplomats to enhance its work. Given scarce resources of money, time, and personnel, it would make little sense for the State Department to have military information and only slightly more sense to have pure economic information.

The DIA, established in 1961, was the result of the U.S. military feeling a need to have more intelligence analysis and collection focused on their needs. The CIA analysts and human intelligence collectors had little motivation for collecting tactical information on Soviet bombers or missiles or order of battle unless it was information to be gleaned for the president and the National Security Council, with the DCI reporting directly to the former. Therefore, DIA was set up by the Secretary of Defense to get a better handle on these military analytical issues to direct the support of the various commands around the world and at home in the Pentagon.

Still, while each department within the IC conducts intelligence analysis and collection based on its own area of expertise, it is also expected to contribute to the overall national assessment of threats, hostile activities by foreign powers, and counterintelligence. Within the IC, there are "centers" of expertise like the NCTC, the National Counterintelligence Center, and others that glean both intelligence and personnel from within the IC.

The operations of such center can be problematic. Not all organizations in the IC are going to agree with these operations on execution and policy. Moreover, they often have separate operations themselves, like the CIA's Counterterrorism Center or various efforts at NSA, FBI, and others investigating cyber-terrorism.

From the charter of pure analysis, the National Intelligence Council and its predecessor organizations were built to provide the president with a single viewpoint on given issues from the IC. The DCI, now DNI, is supposed to sign off on that viewpoint. However, using the right of exception, each agency has the right to object to a specific matter in a specific paper. Sometimes there is general agreement; at other times, a paper can be footnoted to death.

HEADQUARTERS AND FIELD, THE LOCAL GUYS, AND THE PRIVATE SECTOR

Intelligence gathering, as noted elsewhere in this book, is not limited to the IC. Especially with domestic intelligence, there are numerous constituencies involving a large, diverse group of players who try to interact with the federal level.

From the federal standpoint, there is the network of fifty-six FBI field offices around the United States.[3] These offices are charged with collecting counterintelligence and counterterrorism information, and they pass that information back to their National Security Division at headquarters in Washington. Before 9/11, cooperation could be spotty. The case of the Minneapolis field office trying to warn headquarters of Saudis training to fly commercial jets is but one example.[4] In numerous testimonies since 9/11, current FBI Director Robert Mueller assures us that the system has been tightened up.[5]

State and local law enforcement authorities have now joined in the process. With some 17,600 of these entities, the standardization of information collection and analysis has been mixed. Receiving information from the

Homeland Security Information Network, they are often flooded with information and not always sure with whom to coordinate or to whom to pass their information.[6] This is not an insignificant matter.

However, the way that the FBI has reached out to local authorities after 9/11 has been impressive. A good example is the case of the 2005 potential bombing of the tunnels running underneath the harbor in Baltimore, Maryland.[7] Six suspects were captured in the incident. According to multiple U.S. officials, the Baltimore alert was triggered by a report that a shipment of explosives was heading into the city's harbor disguised as cocoa. The explosives then would have been used to build a truck bomb to be detonated inside the tunnel, the officials said.[8] Federal, state, and local authorities began investigating reports of a tunnel plot two weeks before the attack based on shared tips, and police had tactical squads ready to respond to an attack.

Other local departments have decided to strike out on their own. The prime case is that of New York City. Feeling that the federal government efforts were spread too thin and that New York City would be a prime target for any terrorist, Mayor Rudy Giuliani and his successor, Michael Bloomberg, established an unprecedented separate intelligence unit for the city.[9] Numbering more than 350 people, the New York Police Department (NYPD) operates a major headquarters in mid-town Manhattan that performs both collection and analysis.

NYPD also has officers around the world. There are now NYPD officers stationed in London working with New Scotland Yard, in Lyons at the headquarters of Interpol, and in Hamburg, Tel Aviv, and Toronto. There are also two officers on assignment at FBI headquarters in Washington D.C., and New York detectives have traveled to Afghanistan, Egypt, Yemen, Pakistan, and the military's prison at Guantanamo Bay in Cuba to conduct interrogations. Members of the department's command staff have also attended sessions at the Naval War College in Newport, Rhode Island.[10]

The federal government, through the FBI, has worked with a number of state and local authorities to set up The Joint Terrorism Task Forces (JTTF). There are nearly one hundred now around the country. The JTTF is a partnership between various U.S. law enforcement agencies that is charged with taking action against terrorism, which includes the investigation of crimes such as wire fraud and identity theft. The agencies that comprise a JTTF generally include the FBI, other federal agencies (notably DHS components such as U.S. Coast Guard Investigative Service, U.S. Immigration and Customs Enforcement, U.S. Customs and Border Protection, the TSA, and the U.S. Secret Service, as well as the Department of State's Diplomatic Security Service (DSS)), state and local law enforcement, and specialized agencies, such as railroad police.

JTTFs engage in surveillance, electronic monitoring, source development, and interviews in their pursuits. FBI task forces obtain written memoranda of understanding between participating law enforcement agencies. The FBI provides funds to pay for participating agencies' expenses, such as officer overtime, vehicles, fuel, cell phones, and related office costs. One of the criticisms of this JTTF system is that they are haphazardly set up with little control over personnel or training.[11]

There is also an effort, primarily through the auspices of the DHS, to set up "fusion centers." Fusion centers are terrorism prevention and response centers that were started as a joint project between the DHS and the U.S. Department of Justice's Office of Justice Programs between 2003 and 2007.

The fusion centers gather information not only from government sources but also from their partners in the private sector. They are designed to promote information sharing at the federal level between agencies such as the CIA, the FBI, the Department of Justice, U.S. military, and state and local governments. As of July 2009, the DHS recognized at least seventy-two fusion centers. Fusion centers may also be affiliated with an Emergency Operations Center, which responds in the event of a disaster.[12]

State and local police departments provide both space and resources for the majority of fusion centers. The analysts working there can be drawn from DHS, local police, or the private sector. A number of fusion centers operate tip hotlines and also invite relevant information from public employees, such as sanitation workers or firefighters.[13]

The private sector has also launched its own version of intelligence analysis and collection. As former Assistant Secretary for Infrastructure Robert Liscouski estimated in 2004, nearly 85 percent of the nation's infrastructure is held in private hands. As we discussed in Chapter Two, the private sector is using Information Advisory Committees to coordinate their efforts and engage directly with the federal and state and local governments.

The numbers of other measures, such as spending on security guards and spending on physical protection including close circuit television cameras (CCTV), remain sketchy. A Congressional Research Service report from 2004 took a stab at it, estimating there are nearly one million security guards and related personnel in the United States.[14] Private security companies offering CCTV abound.

COOPERATION AND COORDINATION PROBLEMS

Needless to say, cooperation and coordination among seventeen different agencies and all the actors that are charged with protecting American national security is not easy. Divisions and mistrust are an inherent part of any such bureaucracy, yet the IC is an environment that welcomes such a culture due to its very organization and history. The FBI that is headquartered in

Washington may have different motives and goals than the FBI field offices that are stationed throughout the country.

The CIA is reluctant to share all of the information it gathers with the FBI, a division that highlights the difficulties of having two agencies responsible for domestic intelligence with only one of them having police power. The private sector may not want to share intelligence it attains with the federal government out of fear that giving out sensitive information may hurt business and scare away investors.

Much of the hesitance to share information is due not only to inherent mistrust but also legal hindrance. Rules that force classification and denial of access to likely important information prevent many actors in the IC from making accurate and informed assessments when it comes to national security. This makes it all the more challenging to conduct sound domestic intelligence, let alone foreign intelligence.

Indeed, Secretary of Defense Robert Gates has openly stated that our intelligence system is "burdened by 20th century processes and attitudes, mostly rooted in the Cold War. . . . Our counterintelligence procedures are mostly designed to combat an external threat such as a foreign intelligence service."[15] American intelligence institutions have not kept pace with the threat they are supposed to be combating, and much of this is due to the wide array of difficulties of conducting domestic intelligence within the country.

Since 9/11, much of the IC has been focused on increasing the amount of information it shares within its ranks. These efforts were largely the result of the 9/11 Commission, which determined that the cultural and electronic firewalls between intelligence agencies hindered the sharing of information that could have ultimately prevented the attack.

Politicians are quick to recommend more information sharing after a failure of intelligence, such as that of 9/11 or the Christmas Day bombing attempt. Yet political directives can only go so far to change deep-rooted cultures within the agencies of the IC, many of which focus on withholding information rather than making it accessible to other agencies.

Sharing information is also made much more complicated by the fact that intelligence agencies do not have synchronized classification regimes. Each actor within the IC interprets the three classification rules—top secret, secret, and confidential—differently, which limits the amount of information that is even capable of being shared.

This is becoming an increasingly pressing problem not only for agencies in Washington but also for FBI field offices, as the amount of records classified each year has more than doubled since 2001.[16] As an FBI agent in the field, how do you effectively prevent a terror attack when Washington headquarters is reluctant to share information with your office due to classification rules?

This sharing of information is further complicated by information technology (IT) legacy challenges of the 1990s. While it is always fair game to blame the previous guy for your troubles, the IT systems extant in government are definitely one of those long-lasting problems. With little funds for new IT systems in the 1990s, the private sector and the technological advances there did little to pierce the federal government. What systems that were upgraded were often set up on the cheap and were tailored specifically for the customer, who little understood what was happening outside government. In the end, the systems were certainly not set up to talk to each other.[17]

When asked in 2009, the Chief Information Officers of the federal government listed the following as their top problems: security, infrastructure, and system management problems. The Chief Information Officers complained that the "challenges that remain on this list are complex and difficult to fully resolve," and "that is in large part why they have been identified as priority challenges over a period of years."[18] The inability of the FBI to deal with its internal database problems has become an object lesson in these types of troubles.[19]

The culture of secrecy combined with these IT problems has aroused such alarm that, after the Christmas Day bombing attempt, President Obama issued an executive order that mandates the synchronization of classification rules and increased information sharing within and among the IC. Obama's executive order directs federal agencies to use the lowest possible level of classification when it comes to intelligence. While such an effort is laudable, the Christmas Day bombing attempt was not the result of a lack of information sharing, rather just bad intelligence.[20]

In fact, most of the agencies in the IC did share information with each other regarding Umar Farouk Abdul Mutallab: The NSA knew that Al Qaeda had recruited a Nigerian to carry out a terrorist attack some time near Christmas; the State Department had received information from the boy's father that he might have undergone radicalization in Yemen; the CIA even made a background report on Abdul Mutallab.[21] All of this information was forwarded to the NCTC. Yet the NCTC did not act on the information precisely because there was too much of it. The center's 300 analysts are charged with sifting through thousands of reports, intercepts, and tips a day, and determining which ones actually pose a threat to national security is akin to searching for a needle in a haystack.

Furthermore, the bodies that were created to encourage information sharing are simply inundated with so much information that it is difficult to share actionable intelligence in the first place. The Terrorist Identities Datamart Environment, which has information on all suspected domestic and foreign terrorists, has some 550,000 names.[22] The Terrorist Screening Database has 400,000 names (a population that could fit four Rose Bowls), the No-Fly List has 4,000 names, and the mandatory second screening list has 14,000 names.[23] There are thirty such databases; sorting through all of these potential threats is a daunting task. Collecting intelligence is no longer a problem for the IC. It is the analysis and distribution phases of the intelligence cycle that, in an age of terror and the Internet, are the most difficult.

Finally, because the IC is composed of seventeen different agencies, increasing the amount of information they share will not change how they look at the actual intelligence they obtain. Thus, when the State Department gets a report that a Nigerian father is worried about his son being in Yemen, many in the IC could have seen this as a mere consular matter rather than a part of the broader puzzle on Abdul Mutallab.[24] After all, such an intercept does not raise flags and automatically demonstrate a threat to America. This demonstrates that information and the triggers for sharing that information are relative. An organization can claim to have shared information by posting something on its Web site, yet this does not translate into a coordinated threat assessment by the various organizations that compose the IC. All of this indicates that, while information sharing is critical to stopping threats from occurring, it is not a panacea. The IC has a host of other problems that must be dealt with as well for it to have a more effective domestic intelligence system.

INFORMATION HOARDING

Spying is an innately secretive operation, and thus information hoarding happens not only horizontally within the IC but also vertically: from the IC to policymakers and politicians. IC officials are understandably hesitant to share critical pieces of information with high-level policymakers out of fear that they will leak it to other actors not affiliated with the intelligence realm and thus compromise classified material.[25] This, in turn, could threaten the value of a lead and put the entire intelligence operation at risk.

On the other hand, the IC might not share information with the policy-making realm out of fears of creating false alarms and thus compromising its position as an accurate intelligence analysis body. As if the space between intelligence producers and intelligence consumers was not already wide enough, the creation of the DNI in 2004 further added to the hierarchy of the IC. Richard Posner posits that:

> The more layers there are, the less information that will reach the top, where the decisions are made. . . . The additional layer [the DNI] will . . . increase the distance between the producers and the consumers of intelligence, causing potentially dangerous delays even if there is no filtering (but there will also be an increased risk

of misunderstanding), and thus retarding the process by which raw intelligence data become processed into coherent, "actionable" information for policymakers.[26]

The increasing gap between the IC and policymakers compounds the difficulty of gaining accurate intelligence in a timely manner and acting on it. In the post 9/11 world, this weakens America's capability not only of preventing terror attacks but also of responding to them in the event that they do occur.

Furthermore, the very nature of the terror threat makes it hard to track. Because homegrown and international terrorists have access to the Internet, Washington, D.C., is presented with the difficult task of regulating a completely unregulated network. Terror groups like Al Qaeda and its offshoots are versatile and elusive. While they can pull off grand schemes like 9/11, they can also send one man aboard a plane with a bomb in his underpants. Such groups can skillfully conceal their plans, deliberately misinform, and change their strategies right before a planned attack. Terrorists have a wide variety of tools and strategies at their disposal, and thus the American capacity to respond effectively to the terror threat is limited. Political scientist Robert Jervis states:

> To try to build a perfect intelligence system—one that will never miss a terrorist, that intercepts every dangerous email—is an impossibility. We face skilled adversaries who are trying to deceive us. Hiding is often easier than finding. If people are often surprised to discover that their own spouses have been cheating on them, how could we expect governments to have a perfect understanding of what others are doing?"[27]

No matter how much technology and financial expenditures we go through to make our system more impervious to terror, there will most likely always be spaces left for enemies to slip through the cracks. A lot of this has to do with the fact that Washington's financial resources and technological capabilities to combat terror are not unlimited. The limits are evidenced most by the American intelligence in the run-up and in the aftermath of the failed Christmas Day bombing attempt. U.S. border security officials learned of intelligence about Abdul Mutallab and his extremist links when he was en route to Detroit, and planned on questioning him upon his arrival. The decision to wait until he reached the country was made not by choice but by technology. The window for identifying a passenger as a potential threat is limited because in-depth vetting by Customs officials can only begin once the flight manifest has been generated, which is usually just a few hours before takeoff.[28]

After the attack was botched, many government officials speculated whether the United States should fund the deployment overseas of full-body scanners that would have prevented Abdul Mutallab from boarding the plan in the first place.[29]

With each machine costing around $150,000, however, there are many questions about how many we can possibly deploy, where, and how much funding taxpayers will tolerate from politicians who throw money at the threat. Furthermore, President Obama's plan to deploy 300 to 450 of the scanners would cover only a small fraction of domestic airport screening lanes, let alone international airports.[30] Because terrorists can operate in a wide swath of countries as well as on the Internet, it is extremely difficult to apprehend them before they carry out an attack, no matter the technological and financial resources available. This has prompted some experts to say that terrorists by their very nature are undeterrable.[31]

GLOBALIZATION AND TODAY

While the terror threat is becoming more diffuse in accordance with globalization, the way states are responding to that threat is becoming more unilateral. Indeed, it is already difficult to establish standard screening mechanisms for passengers on international flights. Tightening aviation security worldwide requires persuading foreign governments and airports that such measures are necessary for international security. But the terror threat is relative, and as with most matters in international politics, where you stand depends on where you sit. Therefore, other leaders will respond to the threat in ways they deem necessary for their own nations. After the failed Christmas Day bombing attempt, the Obama Administration lobbied allies and airports around the world to adopt common standards for new screening technologies and information sharing about passengers.[32]

But in 2009 the European Parliament rejected the proposal to make the use of whole-body scanners mandatory across the continent.[33] The rejection reflected more immediate concerns about the personal privacy of passengers, as the machines can produce overwhelmingly accurate images of the human body. It also showed the limits of Washington's voice when it comes to coordinating an international response to terrorism:

> Although the United States has authority over airlines that fly to the United States, in practice that power is limited by the willingness of airports and host governments to carry out changes—including paying for new screening machines, making space for them at crowded checkpoints, setting operating procedures, and, ultimately, enforcing the rules.[34]

Other nations have lower criteria for admitting passengers aboard; indeed, not a flag was raised in Amsterdam when Abdul Mutallab paid for a ticket to Detroit in cash and boarded the plane without a single piece of luggage.

Sound domestic intelligence is not merely a government responsibility, but a nationwide task. Washington cannot effectively weed out every terrorist threat on every plane that enters the country, as airlines have much more immediate access to the critical information necessary to prevent such an attack from happening. The private sector, however, is inherently reluctant to disclose information that might affect its business operations. This is especially so in an age when the sharing of information is so heavily emphasized; if passengers find out about potential terror threats on their airline, the financial consequences for the company could be devastating as investors and clients seek other, less risky investments. Michael Chertoff, former Secretary of Homeland Security, has said that "if your [private-sector] partners don't think you'll protect their information, they're not going to be as willing to work with you."[35] Airlines are not the only private companies that are tasked with sharing information with the federal government. As more terror threats are materializing online and targeting corporate Web sites, companies that have extensive operations on the Web are becoming increasingly prone to cyber-attacks.

The new concept of online warfare is becoming increasingly prevalent and is employed not only by terror networks but also by modern nation-states, such as Russia and China. When Google, Inc., came forward in December 2009 alleging that its systems had been breached, intellectual property stolen, and accounts hacked, the biggest surprise was not that the attacks originated from China but that the company chose to disclose the information in the first place.[36] Google was one of thirty-four companies that were targeted in the cyber-attack, and one of only three that came forward with the information.[37]

A similar string of attacks in 2008 against Heartland Payment Systems, Inc., a credit card processing company, resulted in the theft of account information belonging to millions of customers. Three hundred other such companies were targeted, most of which never came forward to disclose the information.[38] Many small businesses simply do not have the capital necessary to withstand customer and investor flight after such an attack. This makes the concept of information sharing among the public and private sector that much more complex.

Perhaps the two most difficult challenges in domestic intelligence are maintaining America's commitment to civil liberties and having a police force that is a criminal investigative unit and a domestic intelligence agency at the same time. Because the former point is discussed extensively in Chapter

Seven, the latter point deserves special mention here. The FBI is a vast internal intelligence organization with both criminal investigation responsibilities and police power. With fifty-six field offices and twenty thousand local police forces that are meant to serve as partners throughout the nation, domestic intelligence has many filters to pass through before it can be effectively communicated among the various levels of the FBI and police force bureaucracy.

Richard Posner has attributed the many weaknesses of the U.S. intelligence system to the entrustment of the domestic intelligence to the FBI.[39] Indeed, the 9/11 Commission agreed, blaming the FBI for the most lackluster performance of any agency in the run-up to 9/11.[40] Since 9/11, the FBI has come under increasing scrutiny as many speculate upon the effectiveness of combining an internal intelligence agency with a law enforcement and criminal investigation body. This is presumably because many American allies throughout the world have sound domestic intelligence agencies that are separate from their national police forces, a subject that will be covered at length in the Chapter Five.

Despite the fact that the work of local law enforcement officials is crucial for obtaining intelligence related to terror attacks and otherwise, the FBI has traditionally been loath to cooperate with local constabularies. Indeed, "many local law enforcers feel deserted by the federal government in general, and the FBI in particular, in regard to national security intelligence. The Bureau does not treat them as partners or even its customers. FBI agents have been known to brush off attempts by local police, and even by other federal officers, to obtain the Bureau's aid in intelligence matters."[41] Such relations do not encourage the sharing of intelligence related to national security.

Because the FBI is at once both a law enforcement and an internal intelligence agency, its capacity to combat the threats of today is inherently limited. The dual missions are often at odds with one another. Cops and spies are two completely separate professions, and often with conflicting interests. Senator Richard C. Shelby, Vice Chairman of the Senate Select Committee on Intelligence, has detailed why, by their very job descriptions, cops are not meant to be intelligence officers:

> Fundamentally, the FBI is a law enforcement organization: its agents are trained and acculturated, rewarded and promoted within an institutional culture the primary purpose of which is the prosecution of criminals. Within the Bureau, information is stored, retrieved, and simply *understood* principally through the conceptual prism of a "case"—a discrete bundle of information the fundamental purpose of

which is to prove elements of crimes against specific potential defendants in a court of law.[42]

Such an institutional culture and emphasis on the "case" is at great odds with the complexities of intelligence gathering. Law enforcement officials are inherently backward looking, focusing on gathering more evidence to make arrests, get convictions, and obtain warrants.[43] Intelligence officials, by contrast, are supposed to be skilled in the art of thinking about the future, connecting disparate pieces of information not for a warrant but to prevent or gain more knowledge of an impending event.

Furthermore, terrorists are not petty criminals but rather mastermind murderers. Their plans cannot be thwarted by the traditional means of criminal investigation precisely because they are much more than criminals. Terrorism is a much more complex transgression than the robbing of a bank: one must possess knowledge of foreign governments, international developments, and unfamiliar languages in order to thwart a terror attack.[44] Cops are trained in a manner that simply does not give them the appropriate set of skills to stop such attacks. In this way, cops do not make good intelligence analysts at all. Police officers are focused on arrests, convictions, media attention, confessions, and hoarding intelligence, whereas intelligence officials prefer anonymity, sustained surveillance to gain more information (rather than impatient arrests), and they know that a single terrorist can cause great harm to the nation, in stark contrast to a criminal.[45]

The differences can be seen in the number of faulty arrests that the FBI has conducted recently in the name of combating terror, one of which included two teenage girls in New York due to suspicions that they were in contact with Al Qaeda and en route to becoming suicide bombers.[46] While the FBI was focused on apprehending the girls, intelligence officials might have tried to penetrate the cell that the girls could have been operating in, so as to gain more valuable information.[47] Lastly, because it is under the jurisdiction of the Department of Justice, the FBI's overriding focus is based on protecting constitutional rights rather than collecting sound intelligence in the name of national security.

THE CHALLENGES AT THE
STATE AND LOCAL LEVEL

There is a saying that all politics are local. For the sake of our argument, all of the federal arguments above can apply to the work being done on domestic intelligence at the state and local level. They even take place in the National Capital Region (NCR), near the center of American government, Washington, D.C.

The City

The first issue in D.C. is who is in charge of homeland security information and intelligence. As *Signal Magazine* noted in a February 2010 article on homeland security challenges for the D.C. police, "Washington, D.C., is rife with multiple federal law enforcement agencies along with other government agencies and organizations that are part of homeland security and counter-terrorism activities. And, as the nation's capital, it is a high-value target for terrorists."[48] It also sits on the border of two states, Maryland and Virginia, and is immediately adjacent to five separate counties.

The biggest concern of Police Chief Lanier, head of the Washington Metropolitan Police (MPD), is that someone will miss the significance of a piece of information and fail to share it with the appropriate authorities. "We still ask the question every day: 'Who needs to know this information and have you shared it with them?'" she says. The same question applies to how well the other agencies share with the MPD. Representatives of the other agencies sit on the MPD fusion center governance board, so the chief hopes that those points of contact ensure proper information sharing from their respective agencies.[49] "Knowing each organization's priorities is essential," she continues. "For example, if the fire department does not know that the MPD needs some information that it routinely collects, that information may not be passed to the MPD when it is needed—and the dots are not connected. So, all parties must make each organization aware of their information needs, or the information sharing capability will fall short of effectiveness."[50]

The MPD's fusion center helps the department achieve its information sharing goals. This facility serves as an information hub that utilizes technology for sharing information. Prior to its establishment, the department relied on liaisons with the various government agencies and law enforcement organizations.[51]

The Feds

Of course, the federal government has a naturally strong interest in securing the region as well. Located bureaucratically, the Joint Forces Headquarters National Capitol Region (JFHQ-NCR), based at Fort McNair in Washington, D.C., is responsible for land-based homeland defense, defense support of civil authorities, and incident management in the NCR.[52]

JFHQ-NCR is responsible for protecting the District of Columbia and neighboring counties and cities of Maryland and Virginia, including Loudoun, Fairfax, and Prince William Counties in Virginia. JFHQ-NCR draws together the existing resources of the Army, Navy, Air Force, Marine Corps, Coast Guard, and North American Aerospace Defense Command (NORAD) into a single headquarters for planning, coordination, and execution of the mission in the NCR.[53]

Other State and Local Entities

To top it all off, there is the coordination effort among and with other state and local entities in the region. In 2002, the DHS stepped in to create the Office for National Capital Region Coordination (NCRC). Under this umbrella, the leadership of the District of Columbia, the State of Maryland, the Commonwealth of Virginia, local area governments, and the DHS's Office for NCRC are working in partnership with non-profit organizations and private sector interests to reduce the vulnerability of the NCR from terrorist attacks. These partners have established a governance structure to guide homeland security work in the NCR (Figure 4.2).[54]

Figure 4.2

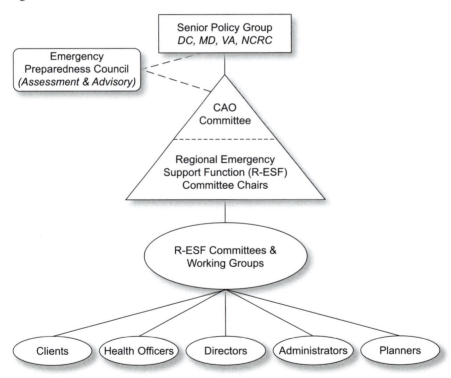

The regional working group and regional emergency support function committees work together to advance preparedness in the region. As the State Administrative Agent for the metro area, the District of Columbia provides management of many of the grant funds allocated to the area. The Metropolitan Washington Council of Governments is the coordination point for many of these activities.

REGION

For federal planning purposes, the NCR region is defined as the following jurisdictions:

- The City of Alexandria
- Arlington County
- District of Columbia
- Fairfax County
- Loudoun County
- Montgomery County
- Prince George's County
- Prince William County[55]

YES, IT IS CHALLENGING

It seems that American intelligence is challenged on a number of fronts. It has problems sharing information. The information it collects is vast. The bureaucracy on the federal level is tangled and designed for another era. State and local authorities are thick on the ground and still need to coordinate with a federal level of government. In many ways, I suppose, it was what the Founding Fathers had in mind. No one gets too much power. But did they want it to be this hard?

In the next chapter we explore a country that seems to have an easier time of it. Some American intelligence experts think it may prove to be a solution to our domestic and national security problems.

5
Chapter

How the British Spy
at Home

One of the first things you hear in conversations about domestic spying in the United States is that what this country needs is an MI-5. Aren't the British like us? They have "common law," and they manage to do pretty effective domestic spying. Even intelligence observer Judge Richard Posner likes the idea. As Posner has said, "We do not have a counterpart to MI-5. This is a serious gap in our defenses."[1] He went on to say, "Primary responsibility for national security intelligence has been given to the FBI. The bureau is a criminal investigation agency. Its orientation is toward arrest and prosecution rather than toward the patient gathering of intelligence with a view to understanding and penetrating a terrorist network."[2]

With all due respect to Judge Posner, I disagree. For some of the other "advocates," I simply say you don't really know the facts of the situation.

In this chapter, we will come to grips with the challenges of domestic spying in the United Kingdom and why this model is not workable in the United States. Stella Rimington, the former head of MI-5, said to the 9/11 Commission that she "doubted the agency would operate under the restrictions of the U.S. Constitution and the traditionally higher American emphasis on civil rights and the right to privacy."[3]

What Rimington was obliquely referencing was the difference between citizen and subject. The fundamental premise of the being a person living in the United States is that we are citizens. A "citizen" is a free individual who enjoys the liberties and privileges of the place in which they reside. A "subject" is someone who is under the power and dominion of another. An American is a citizen. A Briton is a subject.

THE BRITISH CONSTITUTION—UNWRITTEN AND WRITTEN

As a subject of the United Kingdom, unlike a citizen of the United States, you do not have the guarantees of a written constitution as such. This does not mean you are not governed by a system of protective laws. A respected British constitutional lawyer, A.V. Dicey, once wrote that the "twin pillars" of the British constitution are, first, the principle of Parliamentary sovereignty and, second, the rule of law—the common law.

Based on actions as far back as the Magna Charta of 1215 C.E., the former means that Parliament is the supreme law-making body; its Acts are the highest source of British law. The latter is the idea that all laws and government actions conform to certain fundamental and unchanging principles.

Paraphrasing A.V. Dicey, these fundamental principles include equal application of the law; i.e., everyone is equal before the law and no person is above the law, including those in power. Another fundamental principle is that no person is punishable in body or goods without a breach of the law unless there is a clear breach of the law; in other words, people are free to do anything, unless the law says otherwise, thus, no punishment without a clear breach of the law.

In other words, the British system is more "flexible" than the American rule of law. It can adapt more quickly and it is far more subject to the hierarchy of the British class system. In the final analysis, the British are traditionally more willing to let the government into their lives than any American.

A BRIEF HISTORY AND THE PLAYERS

In 1909, the United Kingdom set up the Secret Service Bureau, which was a joint effort of the Admiralty and the War Office. At the time, the war fever that eventually exploded into World War I was gripping the country. The government of Prime Minister Henry Asquith was strongly concerned over rumors of German spies and assistance to Irish nationalists, and he wanted a unit that investigated and tracked these activities both at home and abroad.

This Secret Service Bureau continued until World War I was under way. At that time, given the vast nature of the enterprise in war, the unit was split into what we now think of as MI-5 (domestic) and MI-6 (overseas and focused in Britain's powerful Navy).

MI-5 was named for its position in the Home Office at the Directorate of Military Section 5 and was focused on counter-espionage—finding spies within the United Kingdom. It had no law enforcement authority. That was carried out by its partnership with Special Branch of the London Metropolitan Police. As the largest police department in the largest city in the United Kingdom, the latter provided personnel for arrests and interrogations.

Over the next nearly 80 years until the end of the Cold War in 1991, MI-5 retained that role as chief counterespionage unit. Its role expanded to include Soviet spies and eventually the Irish Republican Army activities in Northern Ireland and the rest of the United Kingdom. Americans often confuse MI-5's research and analytical capabilities with the enforcement activities of the Special Branch—or, more accurately, Special Branches—which are now located throughout numerous cities and support the largest law enforcement jurisdictions in the United Kingdom in cities such as Manchester, Liverpool, Glasgow, etc.

The Special Branches and what they are and do is worth a comment. The first Special Branch was established in London in 1883 under London's Metropolitan Police, and it was tasked with following the agents of the predecessor of the Irish Republican Army. Special Branch was developed to acquire and develop intelligence, usually of a political nature, and to conduct investigations to protect the United Kingdom from perceived threats of subversion, particularly terrorism, and other extremist activities. Special Branch also does some intelligence work; however, Special Branch officers are usually the ones to perform arrests of suspected spies or terrorists, because MI-5 officers are not authorized to take such actions.[4]

MI-5 also enjoys a particularly tight relationship with police forces (constabularies) throughout the United Kingdom—only 53 police forces versus the more than 17,000 in the United States.[5] Because not all of these constabularies have Special Branches, MI-5 has reached out to each one and exchanges intelligence with them on a regular basis, insuring a solid flow of information between the local police forces and the central government.

MI-5 also has a close relationship with the British version of the U.S. NSA, the General Communications Headquarters (GCHQ). Formed after World War II from several different organizations, GCHQ is chartered to conduct signals intelligence operations throughout the world. They also have an extensive domestic relationship with MI-5 dating back to the war. GCHQ has provided substantial amounts of internal British and external signals intelligence to MI-5.[6]

THE OFFICIAL SECRETS ACT

In American sports, we often talk about the game changer. The game changer is the play or action that causes everything to turn around a given way leading the event in another direction. When you talk about spying in the United Kingdom, the Official Secrets Act is that game changer.[7]

The Official Secrets Act of 1889 was passed during Victorian times to limit discussion of classified government information. It is in effect a contract between government employees and the government stating that they will not release such information. As a contract, it is thus enforced. We have nothing like it in the United States.

The Official Secrets Act has been modified on a number of occasions, mostly to cover previous instances of prosecutions that were not covered under the law. In its latest incarnation, the U.K. Official Secrets Act of 1989 declared it unlawful to disclose information relating to defense, security and intelligence, international relations, intelligence gained from other departments or international organizations, intelligence useful to criminals, or the interception of communications.[8]

The origins of the 1989 reform lay in the failure of governments to successfully prosecute under the 1911 Act. In 1985, Clive Ponting, a Ministry of Defence civil servant who had disclosed information on the Falklands War to a Member of Parliament, was acquitted on the grounds that he had disclosed information that the jury had decided was in the interests of the state.

In 1988, the House of Lords—effectively the Supreme Court of the United Kingdom—ruled that the government could not suppress *Spycatcher*, a book written by a former security service employee, Peter Wright, and already published abroad. The ruling was based on a gap in the law that would not punish the publication of these secrets overseas.

In response to the verdict, there were specific categories in the 1989 Act designed to render crucial the nature of information disclosed, leaving motives for disclosure irrelevant, and thus ensuring successful prosecution if such cases arose again. Claims that the 1989 Act can lead to more open government through freedom of information on matters not included in the categories for non-disclosure are generally dismissed on the grounds that the categories for non-disclosure themselves are very broad.[9]

The bottom line for this law is simple: Government information gathering and intelligence analysis are carefully guarded in the United Kingdom, and penalties are imposed if the rules are violated. It is not a system that encourages whistleblowers or litigation.

PLAYERS IN THE POST COLD WAR PERIOD AND BRITISH PUBLIC CONCERN

The ending of the Cold War brought about change in the British internal intelligence system. MI-5 was now spending more effort targeting the Irish Republican Army and other splinter groups. And, of course, they have focused more on home grown Islamic terrorist groups.

There has been a substantial increase in surveillance by MI-5, especially against the Pakistani community in the United Kingdom, with obvious focus on potential Islamic terrorists. This large-scale gathering of information has been done with more than some discomfort within Britain and appears to include a large portion of the general population.

For instance, Member of Parliament Norman Baker accused the British government in July 2006 of "hoarding information about people who pose no danger to (the) country." The information Baker referred to was MI-5's secret files on more than 270,000 people—one in every 160 adults in the United Kingdom.

Moreover, in cooperation with local Special Branch, MI-5 has access to one of the most extensive CCTV networks in the world—nearly 4.2 million cameras throughout the country according to a 2006 report that was presented to the 28th International Data Protection and Privacy Commissioners' Conference in London, hosted by the Information Commissioner's Office.

Richard Thomas, head of the government oversight office, feared the rise of "dataveillance," the use of credit card, mobile phone, and loyalty card information in addition to CCTV. He also noted the rise in "monitoring of work rates, travel, and telecommunications."

Private groups have also expressed concerns over domestic "collection" issues. A group of academics called the Surveillance Studies Network has formed as an independent body established to "promote access to official data and to protect personal details." In their 2006 Report of the Surveillance Society, they have expressed concern over potential government access to keystroke information used to gauge work rates and global positioning sytem information used to track company vehicles.

Still, the overall reaction has been muted, at least by American standards. And the overall amount of collection and the increasing number of CCTV cameras seems to indicate that the trend will not stop soon. An August 2009 report by Privacy International said, "Britain has one and a half times as many surveillance cameras as communist China, despite having a fraction of its population, shocking figures revealed yesterday. There are 4.2 million closed circuit TV cameras here, one per every 14 people."[10]

GOVERNMENT OVERSIGHT OF MI-5

The oversight of the MI-5 by the government has been tightly held for some time. Unlike the United States, with its separation of powers in three equal but separate branches of government, the British system is one in which executive and legislative are parts of a whole. This explains the relatively light touch of U.K. government oversight versus the more rough and tumble version in the United States.

Founded in 1936, The Joint Intelligence Committee (JIC) is part of the British Cabinet Office. It is responsible for directing the national intelligence organizations of the United Kingdom on behalf of the Cabinet of the United

Kingdom (the ruling government) and providing advice to the Cabinet related to security, defense, and foreign affairs.

The JIC also oversees the setting of priorities for the three intelligence and security agencies: the Secret Intelligence Service (MI-6), the Security Service (MI-5), GCHQ, and the Defense Intelligence Service. JIC also establishes professional standards for intelligence analysis in government.

The JIC itself was subject for the first time to oversight by the Intelligence and Security Committee (ISC) established in the Intelligence and Security Act of 1994. The purpose of this act was:

> to make provision about the Secret Intelligence Service and the GCHQ, including provision for the issue of warrants and authorizations enabling certain actions to be taken and for the issue of such warrants and authorizations to be kept under review; to make further provision about warrants issued on applications by the Security Service; to establish a procedure for the investigation of complaints about the Secret Intelligence Service and the GCHQ; to make provision for the establishment of an ISC to scrutinize all three of those bodies; and for connected purposes.

In essence, though, the ISC is still an element of the Cabinet's Intelligence, Security, and Resilience Organization. The ISC itself is chaired by a permanent chairman, usually a Senior Civil Service member (senior permanent government employee).

Additionally, the Prime Minister oversees directly the work of the ISC. Nine members of the group are appointed by the Prime Minister from both the House of Commons and the House of Lords in consultation with the Opposition leader. The reason for this is that, in this capacity, the ISC has greater powers than a select committee of Parliament, being able to demand papers from former governments and provide official advice to ministers, both of which are forbidden to select committees.

While current Ministers are not allowed to be members of the ISC, the ISC reports annually to the Prime Minister, who then lays the report before Parliament, subject to any deletions on security grounds. The ISC also provides ad hoc reports to the Prime Minister from time to time.

THE NEW REALITY OF MODERN BRITAIN
One of the hallmarks of the post World War II period in the United Kingdom was the shift from a nearly 100 percent native-born population to one more ethnically diverse. To Americans, this is part of our culture. We've been doing it for more than 200 years as a nation. As we stand today, nearly 13 percent of our population is not native born. While there is always some

issue of so-called natives versus immigrants, it is expected that all will merge together into some form of "melting pot."

The United Kingdom is much more like continental Europe in terms of its view of itself as a single ethnicity. Thus, Britain has experienced the shock of the new immigrants to the rather insular staid system. In the 2001 census, 8.3 percent of the population (54 million) is now non-native born. Nearly 500,000 people were born in Pakistan. In London itself, now jokingly referred to as "Londonistan," nearly 30 percent of the city's population is foreign born. Nearly 9 percent of the population of London is now Muslim.

Moreover, Britain, unlike the United States, had an immigration policy that allowed lower middle class, blue-collar families from Pakistan to enter the country. The United States tends to attract more upper middle class, entrepreneurial types. This combination of isolation, relative poverty, and high unemployment has provided the United Kingdom with a potent feeding ground for radicalism. A number of madrassas supported by radical Wahhabists from Saudi Arabia have been opened since 2000, teaching both the expectation of the new Muslin Caliphate throughout Europe and the belief in jihad. An example of this rising radicalism is that nearly two thirds of the imams in the United Kingdom, according to the Chief Imam of England, refused to publicly condemn the acts of 9/11 on the United States.[11]

GOVERNMENT REACTIONS TO 9/11

Public reaction in the United Kingdom to 9/11 was sympathetic and anticipatory. There was great outpouring of heartfelt feelings toward America's suffering, and there was increased concern that Britain's own Islamic radicals were becoming increasingly dangerous.

With 9/11 in mind, the government of Prime Minister Tony Blair moved quickly to pass the Anti-Terrorism Crime and Security Act in December 2001. A British version of the U.S.A. PARTIOT Act, this law crossed a number of legal boundaries that subjected it to immediate criticism. Part 4 of the Act allowed for the Home Secretary (essentially the Internal Minister of the United Kingdom) to identify any non-British citizen whom he suspected to be a terrorist and detain them indefinitely, pending deportation, even when such a deportation would be prohibited. In addition, the maximum detention period for someone not charged with a crime was raised from seven days to twenty-eight days.[12]

The House of Lords ruled against the law in a case brought by eight of the detained suspected terrorists on 16 December 2004, and the measure was effectively abolished the following March when it was up for review. However, the old act was soon replaced with the Prevention of Terrorism Act of 2005 in order to satisfy criticisms and add new, helpful legislation.[13]

One of the most powerful parts of the 2005 Act was the so-called "control order." This is an order made by the Home Secretary to restrict an individual's liberty for the purpose of "protecting members of the public from a risk of terrorism." MI-5, the Special Branches, and GCHQ were a deep part of the effort to enforce these broad controls, which include:

- restrictions on the possession of specified articles or substances (such as a mobile telephone);
- restrictions on the use of specified services or facilities (such as internet access);
- restrictions on work and business arrangements;
- restrictions on association or communication with other individuals, specified or generally;
- restrictions on where an individual may reside and who may be admitted to that place;
- a requirement to admit specified individuals to certain locations and to allow such places to be searched and items to be removed there from;
- a prohibition on an individual being in specified location(s) at specified times or days;
- restrictions to an individual's freedom of movement, including giving prior notice of proposed movements;
- a requirement to surrender the individual's passport
- a requirement to allow the individual to be photographed
- a requirement to cooperate with surveillance of the individual's movements or communications, including electronic tagging; and
- a requirement to report to a specified person at specified times and places.

The 2005 Act was no sooner in place than the events of 7 July 2005 occurred.

7 JULY 2005 AND ITS AFTERMATH

The British suffered their worst terrorist attacks in modern history on 7 July 2005; now known as 7/7. On that morning, in the space of an hour, four bombs exploded on London subways and one double-decker bus, killing 56 people including the bombers themselves. An additional 700 people were also injured in the blasts.[14]

The terrorist prevention system that had been carefully designed after America's 9/11 had failed to pick up the individuals or the planning involved in the blast. Subsequent investigation showed that the men involved in the attacks were reported to be "cleanskins," meaning previously unknown to authorities. On the day of the attacks, all four had traveled to Luton in Bedfordshire by car, then to London by train. They were recorded on CCTV arriving at King's Cross station in Central London at about 8:30 A.M. In little over an hour, they had completed their mission.[15]

In response to the bombing, the government immediately ordered that security measures across the United Kingdom rise to the highest alert level. The Times of London reported on 17 July 2005 that police sniper units were following as many as a dozen Al Qaeda suspects in Britain. The covert armed teams were put under orders to shoot to kill if surveillance suggested that a terror suspect was carrying a bomb and he refused to surrender if challenged. A member of S019, Scotland Yard's elite firearms unit, said: "These units are trained to deal with any eventuality. Since the London bombs, they have been deployed to look at certain people."[16]

On 23 July 2005, the police did take action. That day, a Brazilian worker in London was shot to death on the London subway after police believed he was carrying a backpack filled with explosives.[17] The innocent man was identified through profiling by the police and killed with two shots to the head on a filled subway car. The public, still smarting from 7/7, had a mixed reaction from outrage in the minority communities to a more subdued reaction in the general populace more understanding of the error.

After several inquiries, including one classified one, the London Police and their Special Branch were found to "fail to provide for the health, safety, and welfare of Jean Charles de Menezes." The decision not to prosecute individuals was made on the grounds of insufficient evidence. In the end, the London Police and Special Branch paid about $750,000 in fines and offered a terse apology.[18]

WHAT ARE THE DIFFERENCES—UNITED STATES VERSUS THE UNITED KINGDOM?

A Congressional Research Service study in 2003[19] took on the structural question of what in the MI-5 model might work in the United States. The answer was not much. As the study says:

> At the organizational level, the United Kingdom has chosen to separate its domestic intelligence entity (MI-5) from its various law enforcement agencies. The United States, however, has chosen to combine both federal law enforcement and domestic intelligence within the FBI, an agency of the Department of Justice. Each organizational approach is the result of a complex interaction among societal cultures, unique experiences with terrorism, law enforcement and

intelligence organizational cultures, legal precedents, and other factors. A core question involves the possible integration of domestic intelligence and law enforcement functions. Integration may improve coordination of these two functions, but may also undermine the focus and development of skill specialization necessary to succeed in each area.[20]

The cultural question is a deeper one and goes to the heart of the matter. As was mentioned before, America is a nation of laws with a watchful eye out for a centralized government. The United Kingdom has no written constitution as such, with common law established by courts and Parliament as its legal guideline. This reflects the DNA of both countries—untrusting citizen lawyers versus trusting subjects.

This lack of trust, which factors into America's history of litigiousness, has assured a constant scrutiny of American domestic intelligence practices. A barrage of legal action resulted in the exposure of the CIA's and FBI's domestic activities against all forms of dissidents in the 1960s and 1970s, and the pattern of leaking intelligence information is one firmly established in the American psyche—for better or worse.

The British system is far more hide-bound, helped along by a far less litigious society and by the willingness to accept such laws as the Official Secrets Act for more than 100 years. As we discussed before, the Act, with its stiff fines and prison sentences, was enforced seriously for violators. Unlike America, the British have sent the message they expect order in intelligence.

This order also leads to the question of oversight. As mentioned before, the Joint JIC is a rather tightly held organization with relations to the ruling party and the intelligence parties it oversees. The press is particularly circumspect, especially with the looming threat of the Official Secrets Act.

Oversight of intelligence in the United States is, to put it politely, somewhat looser. Congressional oversight resides in House and Senate select committees, with members picked by the leadership. Both committees view their roles as overseers of the U.S. IC with great seriousness and freely dive into budget and program planning, even holding unclassified hearings on issues of interest. The press has no Official Secrets Act to deal with, though selective prosecutions are done on occasion, usually with limited results.

The size issue is also a crucial one. Let there be no mistake—the United States is one big country. With the third largest population in the world and the fourth largest geographic footprint, the United States is truly a giant on the world stage. Add to this sixteen federal agencies devoted to intelligence gathering, 17,600 state, local, and tribal police authorities, and trillions of dollars of infrastructure held by the private sector alone, and you get the picture—a massive, sprawling canvas on which to try to impose some kind of centralized order. For instance, efforts by DHS to guide the development of approximately 70 intelligence fusion centers have met with little success as local police, CIA, FBI, and others join together with little common training or understanding of the total security picture.

As for the United Kingdom, it is relatively small with 60 million people in roughly 90,000 square miles. MI-5 deals with the 90 local police entities and supports the relatively few Special Branches that act as elite police squads devoted to internal threats in cities like London, Manchester, Birmingham, etc. MI-5 and the Special Branches work closely together and have developed a strong system of information sharing with a real cross understanding of the others' needs.

The United States and United Kingdom differ in depth of history as well. Great Britain has had a relatively long history of espionage and attack on its soil. For over one hundred years, the Irish troubles have led to numerous attacks in England and Scotland. The troubles between 1969 and the early 2000s sharpened the skills of those who deal in matters of domestic intelligence gathering and analysis. The recent rise of radical Islam has tested a system already in place to deal with terrorism.

Until recent times, America has had little problem with internal security. The anarchists of the late 19th century presented the greatest security threat, bombing and killing citizens. There were some cases of sabotage in both world wars; hostile religious or nationalist behavior was relatively rare. Thus, the shock of 9/11 to a system where law enforcement and intelligence were meant to be separated by law and practice.

Finally, but not least, the United States and the United Kingdom differ sharply in terms of homogeneity. We are a country of immigrants with some periods of having one in ten of our citizens "foreign born." The idea of a single type of American is not really in our vocabulary. We assimilate.

We have also been relatively selected and relatively lucky in terms of who has immigrated. People who are skilled and upper middle class comprise a fair portion of today's non-Hispanic immigrants. Even the unskilled view the United States as a promised land of work and success, often risking their lives to get here.

The United Kingdom has a much more dour, European attitude toward immigrants. The country had few minorities until the labor shortages after World War II. The new populations tended to be segregated and treated in ways and attitudes that imitated the American South of the mid-20th century. Unemployment among these groups was high. Radical Islamic clerics have found a willing pool of recruits.

WOULD AMERICANS TOLERATE
THE U.K. APPROACH?

In the final analysis, Stella Remington was right. Americans would never tolerate the intrusiveness into their daily lives that the British do with MI-5 and other elements of domestic intelligence gathering.

The American experience, beyond the fundamental difference of citizen versus subject, is also one cluttered with bad feelings from the past. The domestic intelligence activities of the 1950s and 1960s still ring in the mind of the American psyche. The question remains whether time and incident will force America further down the British road.

So what is the bottom line for using an MI-5 model for American intelligence? Not very likely, nor should it be. A combination of psyche, law, structure, and size make it an impossibility. Still, changes need to be made to help us better protect ourselves with better intelligence. The Chapter Six will discuss how we can do just that.

6
Chapter

The Balance of Civil Liberties and Domestic Intelligence

When President Obama took office in January 2009, he said, "As for our common defense, we reject as false the choice between our safety and our ideals." With that statement he appeared to rebuke the Bush Administration's approach to the harsh realities of the war on terrorism and the means used to gather intelligence in defense of the nation.

This tension between the control of government over the individual and the freedom of the citizen is as old as the Enlightenment and extends back to the ancient Greeks. For modern scholars, English philosopher John Locke, one of the founders of Western Liberalism and the basis of the philosophy of our Founding Fathers, was crystallizing discussion in the late 17th century. Ultimately, Locke believed in the social contract between the governing and the governed. The governed had rights that could not and should not be violated. It was up to the government to maintain those rights.[1]

The drafters of our American Constitution, such as Franklin, Jefferson, and Adams, were deeply influenced by Locke. They were men of the Enlightenment, and it showed in the document they produced. Jefferson, prime drafter of the Declaration of Independence, turned Locke's statement on the purpose of man, to be entitled to "life, liberty, and property," into the memorable phrase "life, liberty, and the pursuit of happiness" in the preamble of that Declaration.

Locke also influenced the Founders' view of the control of the state by its people. The power of the state was clearly delineated. The Founders also made clear that the government would be divided into three equal powers, countervailing and meant to oppose one another. Amendments could be added to the Constitution to keep it relevant to the issues of the day, all favoring the rights of the governed. We assume these attributes as part and parcel of our lives. It is a rare and wondrous thing among the nations of the world.

SOMETIMES NOT HONORED IN THE BREACH

The noble aims of the Constitution are honored, for the most part, in peacetime. In a state of war, this has not always been the case. The reasoning often follows the comment of mid-20th century Supreme Court Justice Robert Jackson. Jackson wrote in a dissent on a free speech case, "The choice is not between order and liberty. It is between liberty with order and anarchy without either. There is danger that, if the court does not temper its doctrinaire logic with a little practical wisdom, it will convert the constitutional Bill of Rights into a suicide pact."[2]

Even earlier, in the American Civil War, President Lincoln famously suspended habeas corpus. This was a very serious challenge to the basic principles of the Founding Fathers. A writ of habeas corpus is a judicially enforceable order issued by a court of law to a prison official ordering that a prisoner be brought to the court so it can be determined whether that prisoner has been lawfully imprisoned and, if not, whether he or she should be released from custody.

Lincoln concluded in his role as Commander in Chief that the rebellion required extraordinary measures. Though the order was confined to the State of Maryland and some parts of the Midwest like Indiana, the Presidential Order itself lays out the challenge that a number of Lincoln's successors faced.

> It has become necessary to call into service, not only volunteers, but also portions of the militia of the States by draft, in order to suppress the insurrection existing in the United States, and disloyal persons are not adequately restrained by the ordinary processes of law from hindering this measure, and from giving aid and comfort in various ways to the insurrection. Now, therefore, be it ordered, that during the existing insurrection, and as a necessary measure for suppressing the same, all rebels and insurgents, their aiders and abettors within the United States, and all persons discouraging volunteer enlistments, resisting militia drafts, or guilty of any disloyal practice affording aid and comfort to the rebels against the authority of the United States, shall be subject to martial law, and liable to trial and punishment by courts-martial or military commission.
>
> Second: That the writ of habeas corpus is suspended in respect to all persons arrested, or who are now, or hereafter during the

rebellion shall be, imprisoned in any fort, camp, arsenal, military prisons, or other place of confinement, by any military authority, or by the sentence of any court-martial or military commission.[3]

Although the Supreme Court overruled him in 1862, Lincoln ignored the Court and kept it in place, even reinforcing some aspects of it.[4] Among the 13,000 people arrested under martial law was a Maryland Secessionist, John Merryman. Immediately, Hon. Roger B. Taney, Chief Justice of the Supreme Court of the United States, issued a writ of habeas corpus commanding the military to bring Merryman before him. The military refused to follow the writ. Justice Taney, in ex parte Merriman, then ruled the suspension of habeas corpus unconstitutional because the writ could not be suspended without an Act of Congress. President Lincoln and the military ignored Justice Taney's ruling.[5] Finally, in 1866, after the war, the Supreme Court officially restored habeas corpus in ex parte Milligan, ruling that military trials in areas where the civil courts were capable of functioning were illegal.

That decision was once again challenged during Reconstruction in the South. With near revolt on his hands in South Carolina, President Ulysses Grant also suspended habeas corpus in South Carolina and against members of the Ku Klux Klan. Under the 1870 Force Act[6] and the 1871 Ku Klux Klan Act,[7] the Congress reinforced this action to enforce voting rights for African-Americans in the old Confederacy and made "every person who under cover of any statute, ordinance, regulation, custom, or usage, of any State or Territory or the District of Columbia, subjects, or causes to be subjected, any citizen of the United States or other person within the jurisdiction thereof to the deprivation of any rights, privileges, or immunities secured by the Constitution and laws, shall be liable to the party injured in an action at law."[8] While ultimately regarded as not enforceable, it did give the federal government leeway to crush the Klan and restore order to the South. As we sadly know, however, social practice outweighed for a century Reconstruction legal action.

WORLD WAR II AND THE INTERNMENT OF THE JAPANESE

In February 1942, as American participation in World War II geared up after Pearl Harbor, President Franklin Roosevelt signed Executive Order 9066.[9] This order authorized the Secretary of War and U.S. armed forces commanders to declare areas of the United States as military areas "from which any or all persons may be excluded," although it did not name any nationality or ethnic group. It was eventually applied to one third of the land area of the U.S. (mostly in the Western United States) and was used against those with "Foreign Enemy Ancestry," i.e., Japanese, Italians, and Germans.

The order led to the internment of 120,000 Japanese-Americans in camps throughout the Western United States for the duration of the war. Like the Merriman case during the Civil War, the Executive Order was challenged. In *Korematsu v. United States*,[10] the U.S. government was challenged by an internee who argued his rights had been violated by the Executive Order.

In 1944, the Supreme Court upheld the Executive Order, though it ducked the specific issue of the Japanese-American internment. In the decision, the majority believed the rights of the military to exclude those in designated areas of danger took precedent over the rights of the civilian. However, it also said the "provisions of other orders requiring persons of Japanese ancestry to report to assembly centers and providing for the detention of such persons in assembly and relocation centers were separate, and their validity is not in issue in this proceeding. . . ."[11]

THE GLOBAL WAR ON TERROR AT HOME

The next real national emergency to hit America at home occurred on 9 September 2001. The George W. Bush Administration moved with wartime alacrity in response. Within weeks, the Administration and the Congress began crafting responses to the threat to the American homeland. The Aviation and Transportation Security Act[12] and the U.S.A. PATRIOT Act[13] in late 2001 were the first laws to impress upon the public that the United States was at war.

The Aviation and Transportation Security Act created the TSA, which brought the new rules home to the average American. Immediately, the process of screening all passengers boarding American flights was instituted quickly and overseen by the TSA. The TSA also began cooperating with State Department, CIA, and others to compile No-Fly list, which specifically targeted individuals who might have terrorist connections.

The U.S.A. PATRIOT Act, colloquially known as the "Patriot Act," was the real backbone of the Bush Administration's legal efforts against the terrorist threat at home and abroad. It was also a major step in re-establishing domestic intelligence in the United States.

Within the U.S. borders, the Patriot Act dramatically reduced restrictions on law enforcement agencies; ability to search telephone, e-mail communications, medical, financial, and other records; eased restrictions on foreign intelligence gathering within the United States; expanded the Secretary of the Treasury's authority to regulate financial transactions, particularly those involving foreign individuals and entities; and broadened the discretion of law enforcement and immigration authorities in detaining and deporting immigrants suspected of terrorism-related acts. The act also expanded the definition of terrorism to include domestic terrorism, thus enlarging the number of activities to which the Patriot Act's expanded law enforcement powers could be applied.[14]

While not to the same degree as the suspension of habeas corpus, the Patriot Act modified and expanded a number of domestic government powers. Title I of the act authorizes measures to enhance the ability of domestic security services to prevent terrorism. Title I established a fund for counter-terrorist activities and increased funding for the FBI's Technical Support Center. The military was authorized to provide assistance in some situations that involve WMDs when so requested by the Attorney General. The National Electronic Crime Task Force was expanded, along with the president's authority and abilities in cases of terrorism.[15]

Title II of the Patriot Act, titled "Enhanced Surveillance Procedures," covered all aspects of the surveillance of suspected terrorists, those suspected of engaging in computer fraud or abuse, and agents of a foreign power who are engaged in clandestine activities. It primarily made amendments to FISA and the Electronic Communications Privacy Act. In particular, Title II allows government agencies to gather "foreign intelligence information" from both U.S. and non-U.S. citizens, and it changed FISA to make gaining foreign intelligence information the secondary purpose of FISA-based surveillance, where previously it had been the primary purpose. The change in definition was meant to remove a legal "wall" between criminal investigations and surveillance for the purposes of gathering foreign intelligence, which hampered investigations when criminal and foreign surveillance overlapped.[16]

Title IX amends the National Security Act of 1947 to require the DCI to establish requirements and priorities for foreign intelligence collected under FISA and to provide assistance to the U.S. Attorney General to ensure that information derived from electronic surveillance or physical searches is disseminated for effective foreign intelligence purposes. With the exception of information that might jeopardize an ongoing law enforcement investigation, it was made a requirement that the Attorney General, or the head of any other department or agency of the federal government with law enforcement responsibilities, disclose to the Director any foreign intelligence acquired by the U.S. Department of Justice. The Attorney General and DCI were directed to develop procedures for the Attorney General to follow in order to inform the Director, in a timely manner, of any intention of investigating criminal activity of a foreign intelligence source or potential foreign intelligence source based on the intelligence tip-off from a member of the IC. The Attorney General was also directed to develop procedures on how to best administer these matters.[17]

COLLECTING INTELLIGENCE DOMESTICALLY

The Patriot Act served as a precursor for a number of other efforts supporting domestic spying. Under Executive Order 13354, the Terrorist Threat Integration Center was established.[18] Later renamed the NCTC, the Terrorist Threat Integration Center was to become the single source within the Executive Branch for the collection and analysis of all terrorism intelligence, foreign and domestic. It was explicitly designed to close seams in the terrorist threat–related intelligence process and to provide one organization to gather, assess, and disseminate intelligence information. The Terrorist Threat Integration Center's main purpose was to be a "threat matrix" that delineated on a daily basis the threats to the United States and their potential for happening.

To do this, the Terrorist Threat Integration Center had few of its own personnel and instead drew on a number of agencies, including elements of DHS, the FBI's Counter-terrorism Division, the DIC's Counter-terrorist Center, the Department of Defense, and other U.S. government agencies. While this staffing model was intended to save money, it was also meant to promulgate understanding and education of the effort throughout the diffuse U.S. government community following terrorist threats.[19]

DEFENSE RETURNS TO DOMESTIC INTELLIGENCE

In February 2002, Secretary of Defense Donald Rumsfeld issued Directive 5105.67, which began to move the Department of Defense back into domestic intelligence. The Pentagon's Counterintelligence Field Activity (CIFA) began the TALON/CORNERSTONE database it maintained.

Moving around the Posse Commitatus Act of 1887, a Defense Department background paper for the Directive traces Counterintelligence Field Activity's origins to Presidential Decision Directive 75, "U.S. Counterintelligence Effectiveness—Counterintelligence for the 21st Century," signed by President William Clinton on 5 January 2001.[20] Presidential Decision Directive 75 called for a predictive and proactive CI system with integrated oversight of CI issues across national security agencies. This was interpreted to include the Department of Defense.[21]

Counterintelligence Field Activity's functions, according to the February 2002 directive, were to include:

- evaluating Department of Defense CI activities to determine the extent to which CI policies and resources adequately protect the Department of Defense against the threats of "espionage, terrorism, sabotage, assassination, and other covert or clandestine activities, including those of foreign intelligence services"
- providing CI threat assessments, advisories, and risk assessments to the heads of Department of Defense components;

- providing "tailored analytical and data-mining support" to Department of Defense CI field elements and activities;
- conducting "Domestic Threat Analyses and Risk Assessments"; and
- identifying and tracking "technologies requiring protection."

As the Defense Department announced on 21 August 2007, the TALON/CORNERSTONE database would be terminated while work on new procedures for reporting of threats to the Defense Department and its facilities continues. In the interim, threat reports will be transmitted to the FBI.

The Justice Department, beyond the FBI, was also getting into domestic intelligence. To address "the need for tactical (on the ground) intelligence", the Terrorism Information and Prevention System (TIPS) was created. Set up in January 2002 by Ashcroft's Justice Department, TIPS is described as a "national system for concerned workers to report suspicious activity." In fact, TIPS is a hotline to the National White-Collar Crime Center, a Justice Department organization that deals with "economic crime" and cyber attack. For a little under one million dollars they plan to register all "suspicious, publicly observable activity that could be related to terrorism" and forward it to law enforcement and other agencies "opting to receive TIPS information." These agencies "would be responsible for determining how to respond to the tips they receive."

As we looked at above, the FBI under the U.S.A. PATRIOT Act was able to move ahead in a number of areas. One that stirred debate was the so-called "exigent circumstances letters" that allowed for ex-post explanations of wiretaps. This was originally approved to improve coverage in the cell phone age of disposal phones and Internet communication. However, the record of success appears to be clouded at best.

The FBI collected, according to the *Washington Post*,[22] some two thousand U.S. telephone records invoking terrorist emergencies that did not exist. Half of the more than four thousand toll records collected in emergency situations or with after-the-fact approval were done in technical violation of the law.

One of the most controversial collection of efforts during this period was the Total Information Awareness (TIA), headed by former Reagan Administration official General John Poindexter.[23] Started in January 2002, this effort was assembled in the Pentagon under a group known for its innovate research work, the Defense Advance Research Projects Agency (more commonly referred to as DARPA). The Information Awareness Office was established with the goal of sorting through the vast pile of electronic information. This program would be called Total Information Awareness (TIA).

This TIA "awareness" would be achieved by creating enormous computer databases to gather and store the personal information of everyone in the United States, including personal e-mails, social network analysis, credit card records, phone calls, medical records, and numerous other bits of information, without any requirement for a search warrant. This information would then be analyzed for suspicious activities, connections between individuals, and "threats." Additionally, the program included funding for other methods of gathering information on people, including biometric surveillance, which are technologies that could identify and track individuals using surveillance cameras.[24]

The program did not last long. A combination of internal federal government concerns, the inevitable leaks, and Congressional hearings stopped the program. The final coup occurred in 2003, when the Congress made sure the program was defunded.[25]

There remain a number of programs from this period that continue to leak out. One of interest is NSA cooperation with the private sector, in particular, its access to phones and phone records.[26] According to the leaked information:

> The NSA has been secretly collecting the phone call records of tens of millions of Americans, using data provided by AT&T, Verizon, and BellSouth, people with direct knowledge of the arrangement. . . . [T]he NSA program reaches into homes and businesses across the nation by amassing information about the calls of ordinary Americans—most of whom aren't suspected of any crime. This program does not involve the NSA listening to or recording conversations. But the spy agency is using the data to analyze calling patterns in an effort to detect terrorist activity, sources said in separate interviews.[27]

THE ECHELON PROGRAM

For years, the more paranoid among us had insisted that the government was listening in on all of our calls and storing them away for use against us. Well, this group was not comforted by news that began to break in late 1999 about an electronic spying system called Echelon. The British Broadcasting Corporation (BBC) called it a "global spying network that can eavesdrop on every single phone call, fax or e-mail, anywhere on the planet."[28] According to the BBC and other press reports, Echelon was created to monitor the military and diplomatic communications of the Soviet Union and its Eastern Bloc countries during the Cold War. However, it is now used purportedly to search also for evidence of terrorist plots and drug organization activities.[29]

The BBC went on to contact the two of the chief protagonists, the United Kingdom and the United States, and they officially deny its existence. But the BBC did get "confirmation from the Australian government that such a network really does exist and politicians on both sides of the Atlantic are calling for an inquiry.

As the European Parliament later ferreted out in two reports in 2000 and 2001, Echelon was signals intelligence collection and analysis network operated on behalf of the five signatory states to the U.K.–U.S.A. Security Agreement (Australia, Canada, New Zealand, the United Kingdom, and the United States). It was described as only a software system that controls the download and dissemination of the intercept of commercial satellite trunk communications.[30] The report also said that interception of private communications by foreign intelligence services is not necessarily limited to the U.S. or British foreign intelligence services.

The report stated that Echelon was capable of the interception and content inspection of telephone calls, faxes, e-mail communications, and other data traffic globally through the interception of communication bearers including satellite transmission, public switched telephone networks, which once carried most Internet traffic, and microwave links.

NSA expert and author James Bamford came to the same conclusions in his book on electronic spying in 2002.[31] Bamford describes the system as the software controlling the collection and distribution of civilian telecommunications traffic conveyed using communication satellites, with the collection being undertaken by ground stations located in the footprint of the downlink leg.

Whatever its shape, size or name, neither the NSA nor GCHQ has ever admitted or denied its existence.

THE PRIVATE SECTOR SPIES WITH GOVERNMENT CONNECTIONS

The history of America is filled with tales of detective agencies, from the Pinkerton Agency to the modern day Kroll, who engaged in private investigation, and security services including background screening, business intelligence, market intelligence, forensic accounting, electronic discovery, and data recovery.[32] The market for this private service is quite large and quite legal. Anyone who has ever had a background investigation to get a job in the private sector or the government knows that a number of these companies exist. They tend to keep their size and clients secret.

However, once in a while a good analysis of the industry is put together. *Fortune* Magazine in 2004 did an extensive investigatory piece outlining some of the secrets.[33] It was estimated at the time that overall spending on corporate security and intelligence could reach $50 billion this year . . . includ(ing) physical security, Internet safeguards, staff screening and training, and competitive intelligence, not just terrorist and related intelligence analysis.[34]

The article also noted the growing involvement of former government security personnel in private security. "Many of these private intelligence analysts were trained by the CIA, the FBI, or the military or in spy organizations in Russia, Israel, and other foreign lands."[35] A growing trend for large corporations is ". . . hiring or contracting with intelligence veterans. Lehman Brothers, for example, brought in Ted Price, former deputy director of operations at the CIA, to be its head of global corporate security after 9/11. Senior security executives at big corporations meet regularly with local and national intelligence and law-enforcement agencies."[36]

Companies have also engaged in large-scale information collection and analysis on American citizens—selling some to the federal government. One of the largest, for instance, is a company called ChoicePoint. Spun off from another security firm in 1997, ChoicePoint combines personal data sourced from multiple public and private databases for sale to the government and the private sector. In 2005, the firm maintained more than 17 billion records of individuals and businesses, which it sold to an estimated 100,000 clients, including 7,000 federal, state, and local law enforcement agencies.[37]

On its Web site, ChoicePoint advertises a system that is ". . . is as easy as point-and-click. Using . . . powerful search capabilities, you can easily browse through billions of current and historical records on individuals and businesses. Whether you're investigating fraud, conducting criminal and civil investigations, locating witnesses, finding missing children, or locating and verifying assets, (the service) can deliver comprehensive information right to your desktop."[38]

The federal government does have restrictions placed on it by various laws enacted over the last 30 years. The Private Act of 1974[39] and The Computer Matching and Privacy Protection Act of 1988[40] lay out the rules for how federal agencies may acquire information from private databases and by their own means. In theory, both laws are intended to provide individuals with broad protection from the unauthorized use of records that federal agencies maintain about them. It requires agencies to account for disclosures of records that it maintains, and to take steps to minimize and protect the accuracy of records. It also requires agencies to reveal the purposes for which they are collecting information, and it gives individuals a right to gain access to records about them. Individuals may sue in federal District Court if their rights under the Privacy Act are violated, and there are criminal penalties for knowing and willful violation of the Act.[41]

In the private sector, the rules are far more limited.[42] In 2006, the Government Accountability Office reported to the Senate Committee on Banking, Housing, and Urban Affairs that:

. . . the applicability of the primary federal privacy and data security laws—the Fair Credit Reporting Act (FCRA) and Gramm-Leach-Bliley

Act (GLBA)—to information resellers is limited. FCRA applies to information collected or used to help determine eligibility for such things as credit or insurance, while GLBA only applies to information obtained by or from a GLBA-defined financial institution. Although these laws include data security provisions, consumers could benefit from the expansion of such requirements to all sensitive personal information held by resellers.

The report also noted that the Federal Trade Commission did not have civil penalty authority under the privacy and safeguarding provisions of GLBA, which may reduce its ability to enforce that law most effectively against certain violations, such as breaches of mass consumer data. The report also reviewed state laws and concluded that the situation was no better at that level.[43]

EFFORTS TO OVERSEE DOMESTIC SPYING

While government domestic spying efforts were flourishing post 9/11, the Bush Administration did put into place some mechanism for overseeing the process.

Under Executive Order 1335 in August 2004, the President's Board on Safeguarding Americans' Civil Liberties was established. A recommendation of the 9/11 Commission was meant to advise the president periodically about "federal departments and agencies relating to policies and procedures that ensure implementation of the Policy." With the Deputy Attorney General as chair, the committee was filled with senior Justice Department, DHS, and FBI and IC officials. It was also empowered to take:

> steps to enhance cooperation and coordination among federal departments and agencies in the implementation of the Policy, including but not limited to working with the Director of the Office of Management and Budget and other officers of the United States to review and assist in the coordination of guidelines and policies concerning national security and homeland security efforts, such as information collection and sharing; and . . . undertake other efforts to protect the legal rights of all Americans, including freedoms, civil liberties, and information privacy guaranteed by federal law, as the President may direct.

Additionally, an office was established in 2003 within the DHS to reinforce oversight of the global war on terror at home. The Office of Civil Rights and Political Liberties examined the legal treatment of aliens in connection with national security investigation. Moreover, it reinforced the Attorney General's guidelines regarding racial profiling in law enforcement activities. By 2004, the office had received 55 cases complaining of mistreatment.

So, after much recent action and with past precedence, it is easy to see why the argument about the freedoms of the citizen and the state at war continues. There are many viewpoints, but they seem to have crystallized around the defenders and the critics of the approach of the Bush Administration.

Mark Theissen, former speechwriter for President George W. Bush, has been vehement in his support of the tough standards when a democracy is confronted by terrorism. It is, to Theissen, a case of use of tactics to prevent the next attack on American soil.[44]

Theissen argues, for example, that the NSA's program to monitor foreign terrorist communications at home and abroad is a good one. He is strongly concerned that in the Senate, President Barack Obama voted against confirming then-NSA Director Michael Hayden to lead the CIA because, in Obama's words, Hayden was "the architect and chief defender of a program of wiretapping and collection of phone records outside of FISA oversight."

Others, like former Hill Staffer and CIA Assistant General Counsel Suzanne Spaulding, are concerned that the balance of civil liberties and domestic intelligence collection are becoming skewed over time.

> In a traditional kind of war, where we know it's going to have an end at some point, we may be able to live with that skewing of the normal checks and balances. One of the reasons it's of such concern when this authority is asserted in the context of this global war on terrorism is that we are also told that this war will last likely through our lifetimes, our children's lifetimes, perhaps our grandchildren's lifetimes. The question we have to ask ourselves is, do we really want that system of checks and balances to be skewed for that long a period of time?[45]

THE NEW PRESIDENT REVIEWS

The Obama Administration was elected seven years after 9/11. The ardor of the early Bush years had tempered, and people in the Obama Administration viewed the struggle as less a war than a long-term conflict, perhaps more police action than war. This immediately led to questions about the kind of domestic intelligence we needed to spy on enemies at home. And what safety measures needed to be taken to make sure they did not impinge on civil liberties.

While the current National Security Strategy review by the Obama Administration has yet to be released, it is unlikely that the approach will change significantly from the previous administration. Hints of this were scattered during the 2008 campaign. As FISA renewal came up, for instance, Obama made it quite clear that "the ability to monitor and track individuals who want to attack the United States is a vital counter-terrorism tool, and I'm persuaded that it is necessary to keep the American people safe."

Out of the heat of election, Attorney General Eric Holder's initial efforts to prosecute those who had been involved in enhanced interrogation techniques where stifled rather quickly with a White House review and subsequent reversal. At both FBI and DHS, the leadership continues to support strong intelligence efforts.

Even the personnel involved in the process are either experienced intelligence hands or those who quickly fell in line with a continued aggressive policy. For instance, John Brennan, the Bush head of NCTC, became Obama's chief NSC counter-terrorism advisor. Michael Leiter, currently head of NCTC, was a Bush Administration holdover, and CIA head Leon Panetta has proven to be a vehement defender of the CIA.

THE NEW FRONTIER OF CYBERSPACE

In a new development, the issue of cyberspace is finally being addressed. The White House released a comprehensive report on cyberspace defense in spring of 2009.[46] The bottom line of the report was that the United States was ill prepared to deal with both the potential offensive and defense nature of threats in the cyber world. Furthermore, there was a recommendation to appoint a "czar" or at least a single point of operational contact for the issue—someone within the federal bureaucracy who could take charge. It was not the first time the issue had been considered.

The issue of cyber security and the U.S. government's role has been around for some time. Back in 1997, the nascent Internet was the subject of a Supreme Court case over content.[47] The Supreme Court ruled that government interference in the net was not going to be allowed. The battle over content and access issues has been going on ever since.

The White House report, however, comes in a time of both quasi-war and a time when the military and the public are becoming more and more dependent on the Internet for day to day activities. The U.S. military, for instance, talks of net-centric warfare—using the Internet's speed and throughput to move information to the right people at the right moment in action.

For the civilian part of the population, few of us can count a moment now when we don't do electronic banking or buy something from eBay on the Internet. And what of the billions of communications that occur through the Internet, twitters and other social web sites every day?

So, the worries of the federal government are well placed. The U.S. military is vulnerable to Internet attacks by hackers of any stripe, from government spies overseas to angry 15-year-olds in basements and bedrooms around the world. As for the public sector, the social sites and the emails also contain messages for those that mean us harm. The incidents at Fort Hood and Times Square only reinforce this concern.[48]

With that concern, the NSA has been placed in the lead of the new cyber-terrorism effort.[49, 50] Veteran military signals man General Keith Alexander is about to take the NSA and the rest of the federal government into a comprehensive form of reviewing the net. He is also going to try to prevent terrorists from using the Internet with impunity. And he is going to try to wrangle any number of interested and active players in the federal government from CIA to DHS to FBI.

So with FISA rules still somewhat ambiguous, exactly what can you do about cyberspace? From the ever important bureaucratic standpoint, Alexander heads the largest agency in the federal government dealing with cyber issues and certainly the most competent. The NSA was developed to work with signals intelligence monitoring. It has, in recent years, expanded into the Internet as we discussed before in the section on FISA and "warrantless taps."[51] On that last point, a number of Americans are more than a little concerned over a spy agency doing such work—even former, high-level government employees active in the area. [52, 53]

They are even less happy to have an agency that is part of the military doing it. The Cyber Command, as it will be called, will be part of the U.S. military. The U.S. Cyber Command (USCYBERCOM) is a subordinate unified command under U.S. Strategic Command, which was created by Defense Secretary Robert Gates on 23 June 2009 and activated in September of that year. The command will assume responsibility for several existing organizations within the military. The Joint Task Force for Global Network Operations and the Joint Functional Component Command for Network Warfare will be dissolved by October 2010. The Defense Information Systems Agency will be moving its headquarters to Ft. Meade and will provide technical assistance for network and information assurance to USCYBERCOM.[54]

The mission of USCYBERCOM is to coordinate computer-network defense and direct U.S. cyber attack operation. This came in response to repeated reports of attacks on U.S. defense networks, including a breach reportedly of the U.S. electricity grid and of the F-35 fighter jet program.[55]

Coordination among all the currently involved government agencies is also problematic, with FBI, CIA, and DHS each having a piece of the vast cyberspace challenge. However, General Alexander, the newly selected USCYBERCOM head, thought he could overcome this conflict. "NSA already has been invited by several agencies to help them secure networks." Alexander says NSA has done that for many years. "We are the national manager for national security systems and in that regard we have responsibility to help all federal agencies that have national security systems," he says.[56]

For his part, President Obama moved to tamp down concerns about the new USCYBERCOM. Obama was quick to add that the new White House cyber security office would include an official whose job is to ensure that the government's cyber policies don't violate the privacy and civil liberties of Americans. He also reaffirmed his support for the principle of net neutrality. "Our pursuit of cyber security will not include—I repeat, will not include—monitoring private sector networks or Internet traffic," he said. "We will preserve and protect the personal privacy and civil liberties that we cherish as Americans. Indeed, I remain firmly committed to net neutrality so we can keep the Internet as it should be, open and free."[57]

HOW DO YOU ARREST A TERRORIST?

As we discussed earlier, there was a sweeping series of laws put in place during the Bush Administration to deal with all forms of terrorism. We need to get them off the streets and we need their information for our intelligence. But, a troubling issue arises frequently in our continuing battle against terrorism—how do you treat Americans who are terrorists?

Simplistically, under the Constitution and following clarifications and modifications of the Supreme Court, a defendant has a right to counsel. The Sixth Amendment to the Bill of Rights makes it quite clear:

> In all criminal prosecutions, the accused shall enjoy the right to a speedy and public trial, by an impartial jury of the state and district where in the crime shall have been committed, which district shall have been previously ascertained by law, and to be informed of the nature and cause of the accusation; to be confronted with the witnesses against him; to have compulsory process for obtaining witnesses in his favor, and to have the Assistance of Counsel for his defense.

Court cases over the years have parsed the words and provided expanded meaning for the Right to Counsel. One, in particular of interest for us, is the so-called Miranda Decision. In the 1966 case *Miranda v. Arizona*,[58] the Court held that both inculpatory and exculpatory statements made in response to interrogation by a defendant in police custody will be admissible at trial only if the prosecution can show that the defendant was informed of the right to consult with an attorney before and during questioning and of the right against self-incrimination prior to questioning by police, and that the defendant not only understood these rights, but voluntarily waived them.[59]

In 2001, the Bush Administration had to face the awkward fact than an American citizen could be a terrorist. The initial rules set in place by the

Administration said that an arrested terrorist would be foreign and was to be considered an enemy combatant. No Miranda rights were read and they were kept in confinement without habeus corpus with the total effort of their incarceration focused on the gathering of information. The Padilla case was a fine example of this challenge.

Jose Padilla was from Chicago and had changed his name to Abdullah Al-Mahsajir. On 8 May 2002, Padilla was arrested as a material witness against Al Qaeda after strong information that his travel to Pakistan and Afghanistan had put him in contact with the terrorists who executed 9/11 and wanted to blow up a dirty bomb in New York City. Upon the recommendation of his counsel, President Bush ordered Secretary of Defense Donald Rumsfeld to place Padilla under arrest as an enemy combatant.[60]

As a U.S. citizen, Padilla is entitled to certain rights. Had the rules shifted under the new war on terrorism? After years of appeals by both Padilla and the federal government, the answer was given. On 3 April 2006, the U.S. Supreme Court declined, with three justices dissenting from denial of certiorari, to hear Padilla's appeal from the 4th Circuit Court's decision that the president had the power to designate him and detain him as an "enemy combatant" without charges and with disregard to habeas corpus.[61]

This refusal to grant "cert" was no random statement. It confirmed a Supreme Court decision in 2004 called *Hamdi v. Rumsfeld.*[62] As the *Washington Post* noted in a 9 May 2009 op-ed, government had the right to hold as an enemy combatant a U.S. citizen who was captured fighting for the Taliban in Afghanistan. The court left intact a World War II–era decision that allowed the government to prosecute as an enemy combatant a U.S. citizen who was captured on U.S. soil while part of a Nazi sabotage operation.

With the coming of the new Obama Administration in 2009, there was a marked shift in attitude toward American terrorists. In particular, Attorney General Eric Holder decided to review the policy to determine what course of action to take—treat the terrorists as law enforcement cases or treat them as enemy combatants. The cases in Detroit and Times Square put the policy to the test—law enforcement first. The shift in policy caused controversy on left and right.

As the *Washington Post* in a critical op-ed said,

> The Obama Administration's response to attempted acts of domestic terrorism has been consistently conventional: Suspects are apprehended, perhaps questioned under a public-safety exception to Miranda rights and then read their rights hours later and charged in a civilian court. This was the pattern followed with the Nigerian man accused of trying to blow up an airplane over Detroit on Christmas Day and with Faisal Shahzad, the U.S. citizen

charged with trying to detonate a car bomb last weekend in New York's Times Square."

There has been strong concern, however, whether this change in policy will affect our ability to collect information from these suspects. More than a few people have argued that naming these Americans "enemy combatants" would allow just that. Senator John McCain, Ranking Republican member of the Senate Armed Services Committee and former opponent of President Obama in 2008, said as much for the opposition. McCain, speaking bluntly on a widely watched talk show, said, "Don't give this guy his Miranda rights until we find out what it's all about."[63]

Even the fairly liberal *Washington Post*, in the 9 May 2010 op-ed, opined that "that the administration has not given more consideration to other approaches, including the possibility of designating suspects as enemy combatants to allow for lengthier interrogations, which could yield intelligence to thwart terrorist operations and future attacks."

In the final analysis, this debate is simply part of a much longer debate about what is and what is not allowed in time of war. However, this war is a hotter version of the Cold War. It is near-war; an unconventional war. The rules are still shifting and changing. The rules to collect information from citizens through interragation or via spying on the net will also shift over time. That is the nature of the public opinion and the body politic.

What is not going away soon is the terrorist threat to America. In Chapter Seven, we will discuss how to deal effectively with this generational problem.

7 Chapter

The Next Steps in American Domestic Intelligence

In the course of any book, you can lose perspective on what the author is talking about. So to be quite clear to the reader, I believe the following:

1. The threat of Islamic terrorism against the United States is not going away soon—likely for a generation—and the number of attacks in our homeland will rise in unprecedented numbers.
2. This prospect means we need to protect ourselves sensibly, and the front line of that sensible protection is more and better domestic intelligence organization, the collection and sharing of information and analysis.
3. To be effective, domestic intelligence is going to be more intrusive and more pervasive than we have seen outside of previous "normal times."
4. We must be ever vigilant through effective oversight to make sure the errors of the past are not repeated and our civil rights are defended within reason.

Like many of us, I was at home watching television the morning of 9/11. I looked up from the paper just in time to see the second plane crash into the World Trade Center. Two thoughts raced through my head in the next half hour. First, after the Pentagon attack, was my wife safe—she was and came home from her government office rather shaken.

The second thought I had was that we were in for a long, bloody war like many parts of the rest of the world. My friends and I in various places around Washington, D.C., had predicted an attack for so long. The Hart-Rudman report issued in February 2001 made no bones about an attack

happening on U.S. soil.[1] The scale and breath of the attack surprised even
the most pessimistic of us.

Whatever thoughts I had in the next few days lay in what our response
would be and why our intelligence had failed to pick this up. Only later did
we see that American intelligence had picked up something—but picked it
up in a way in which it was relatively useless to the policymakers and certainly not helpful to law enforcement authorities.[2]

In the final analysis of both the 9/11 Commission and the WMD Commissions, the failure to pick up the events of that awful day in September
was not the result of stupid people. It was the result of a system that had
been formulated in the Cold War against the Russians. It was an intelligence
system that worked best against a nation-state that looked and acted more
Western than not. While based on an ideology, the former Soviet Union had
a high, Western regard for human life and a wariness of headlong attacks
against its enemies, preferring war by proxy.

Bin Laden and Al Qaeda (meaning "The Base" in Arabic) were a new
creation quite different from the old enemy.[3] Effectively founded in 1988, Al
Qaeda took advantage of the modern technologies such as the Internet to
spread its message. Tied neither to a large structure nor a "command center,"
they could conduct training at various bases in Afghanistan and western
Pakistan, where the governments were either friendly or could be controlled.
They were willing to "franchise" operations with loose control and affiliation
with and over like-minded groups elsewhere in the world.

Al Qaeda embraced a romantic form of Islam, an Islam that was taking
root among those who regarded themselves as true believers fighting against
the continued modernization of Islam. Al Qaeda embraced the idea of a
return to the 14th century and the historic Caliphate extending from Spain
through Indonesia. The United States, in many ways, was collateral damage
to this ideological "food fight" within Islam. However, Washington's backing
of pro-Western ideology, pro-Western regimes in the Middle East and Israel
made it target number one for Bin Laden.

The combination of a non-nation state enemy, free movement across
the boundaries of cyberspace, and a belief structure based on religion threw
American intelligence for a loop. Suddenly, or perhaps not so suddenly given
a ten-year build up of actions, we faced an enemy far different than the
Russians with a structure of intelligence that was in no way able to deal with
this new brand of enemy effectively.

FIRST, ADMIT THE PROBLEM

The first step in any addiction program is to admit you have a problem.
And America, when it comes to its domestic intelligence has a big problem.

As Judge Richard Posner noted in 2005,[4] "The goal of national security intelligence is to prevent a terrorist attack, not just punish the attacker after it occurs, and the information that enables the detection of an impending attack may be scattered around the world in tiny bits. A much wider, finer-meshed net must be cast than when investigating a specific crime. Many of the relevant bits may be in the e-mails, phone conversations or banking records of U.S. citizens, some innocent, some not so innocent. The government is entitled to those data, but just for the limited purpose of protecting national security."

The federal government and all the state and private organizations are still ill organized to collect this crucial data. America is sitting nearly nine years after 9/11 with a domestic intelligence system that is at best patched together. Those who claim its success note that nothing has happened on U.S. soil since that horrific day. Yet, there is a mounting threat of a loose connection of radicals and "nut cases" who are using the Internet to connect and breed. The incident at Fort Hood, the Underpants Bomber, the Times Square failure, and cases like Jihad Jane are but the tip of an ever-growing iceberg that is just starting to bite us.

As we spoke about in the first chapter, intelligence is a difficult process. It is not simply the collection of information, but coalescing that information into a comprehensive form that provides context. It is also subject—to put it politely—to interpretation. Just because you provide insightful analysis does not mean the policymaker will use it.

Domestic intelligence comes at an even higher price. As the Constitution makes so amply clear, the American DNA rejects monolithic, intrusive government. We are citizens, not subjects. And domestic intelligence smacks of a government looking to dig into the private business of its citizens. Such efforts are not to be trusted.

Still, Americans are realists. The attacks of 9/11 and other attempts since that day remind the public that there are dangers out there far beyond what have experienced in most of our history. The litany of these dangers is long and growing longer by the day. And the lack of real borders in the age of universal travel and borderless cyberspace is enhancing those dangers.

Despite these dangers, our history with domestic intelligence is spotty. We never really had international intelligence in a comprehensive form until after World War II. Domestic intelligence was performed mostly by the FBI before World War II. However, during the thirty years following the War, the FBI, CIA, and others well exceeded their brief to protect the people of America from communism by spying on all types of dissidents. Even in the face of 9/11, those memories still linger, and when they are combined with the DNA of our fear of big, intrusive government, we are not likely to ease our wariness any time soon.

Consequently, what we have set up to conduct domestic intelligence is a spotty, hodgepodge of organizations based mostly on Cold War instruments. From 1947 through 2004, no major changes were made to the American IC except to add organizations devoted to dealing with news problem. Even after 9/11, most of the changes were of the same approach. The Iraq WMD analytical failure resulted in another layer of bureaucracy on top of federal intelligence. Coordination among the bodies remains problematic, and the government coordination with private and state and local authorities outside the Beltway is abysmal.

Some suggest the British model as the solution to our current difficulties. We hear about the benefits of an MI-5. Most who suggest this have no clue about what MI-5 does and how it fits into the British system of common law and small size. With a population of 60 million people in 90,000 square miles, the United Kingdom has no more than 90 or so local police authorities. In the United States, we have 17,000 focused on more than 300 million people living in over 3.8 million square miles. In addition, those who advocate the British system of domestic intelligence do not understand the difference between being an American citizen and being a British subject. Even their domestic intelligence head admits that Americans would never tolerate British intrusiveness.

Americans value their civil liberties. But, we have had plenty of limited instances where we were willing to forgo some of them for a while during national crisis. We have even been willing to suspend habeas corpus during the worst of the crises. However, it is now clear that this will be a generational conflict and that the early rules established to keep us safe may be open to some question. That being said, the Obama Administration is playing cautious, as no party in power wants a new 9/11 on their watch.

Bottom line: America needs good domestic intelligence. This is not going to be easy. Solutions to problems are not always going to be effective. The work is going to be hard. Adjustments need to be made constantly. There will be screw-ups. We need to be vigilant of our rights, which history shows can be easily trampled without due diligence.

STEP ONE: TELL AMERICANS THE TRUTH

The hardest thing for any politician to do is address the truth of a situation. Not illogically, they live and die by the vote, and they want their voters to be happy. And the truth in this case will likely not make the voters ecstatic. Still, American history indicates they can handle the truth.

Americans were willing to accept a Cold War that lasted some 50 years. They argued over strategies and tactics. They condemned, overreacted, and sometime clearly missed opportunities. But they also understood that the sacrifice was necessary. Our enemy is implacable, and so must we be. History shows that all these types of terrorist actions last thirty to fifty years.

We may whine and complain, but I think the American public accepts that some inconvenience and intrusion is necessary for its safety. Anyone who has stood in line at an airport has seen that spirit. The queues are orderly; the people are hardly in revolt. It may seem corny in today's age of cynicism, but I believe President Kennedy was right in his 1961 inaugural address referring to Communism: We are willing and able to "pay any price, bear any burden, meet any hardship, support any friend, oppose any foe, in order to assure the survival and the success of liberty."

The public must know that, whatever we are spending on homeland security and the domestic intelligence to support it, there are going to be people and incidents that get through the system. Part of this is due to an adaptable enemy who sees our strategies and adapts accordingly. As Mark Levitt, head of the Stein Program on Counterterrorism and Intelligence at The Washington Institute for Near East Policy:

> The startling and depressing truth is that eight years after Sept. 11, we cannot say with confidence that we are likely to prevent the next attack here. The reason is not insufficient attention, resources or effort. It's the fact that there is no such thing as 100 percent success in counterterrorism.[5]

Al Qaeda, the Taliban, and the like know that large-scale conspiracy is increasingly difficult to maintain. Operational activities and the inevitable slip-ups among those with loose lips and clumsy security practices is a dead giveaway. So, they will now go into the vast frontier of cyberspace and recruit the individual. The ideal recruits are those people who are angry, dissatisfied, or are looking for something to believe in are harder to detect and ultimately defend against.

But, we must also make it clear to the public that Al Qaeda is smart. They will change their strategies and they will probe us to find out information about our work. As in the case of Times Square, the vigilant citizen is sometimes the best weapon we have.

STEP TWO: DEFINE THE PROBLEM

One of the challenges of dealing with a corporation or government is that people want to solve the problem without looking at the problem or thinking about what the problem truly is. In organization speak, complex problems tend to quickly become "wicked problems." Not only are they problems without immediate solutions, they remain problems because there is a "suboptimal solution" at best and the very people involved in solving the problem are part of the problem.

So who is the enemy that domestic intelligence must seek out, and what are they trying to do? The enemy as I have defined it is a form of radical Islam that takes many shapes. Al Qaeda has franchised this anger and is its leading proponent. It does exercise some influence via the Internet and public propaganda. There is, however, no "Dr. No" overseeing the process. Nor is it just a bunch of guys in caves in Afghanistan/Pakistan doing their best to inflame the angry and dissatisfied.

We are now dealing with a new kind of state—the non-state. It is fluid and amorphous. The edge it has taken advantage of is cyberspace. Here it can find like minds and recruit them to the cause. The question of what the organizational title is or where it is and who belongs is a 20th century concept.

The ideology here is the key to understanding it. Al Qaeda, and others like the Taliban, are reaching out to the disaffected of modern times. They are reaching out to those who wish to be part of something greater than them. We may adjudge these people to be loners, or "nut cases," or whatever vituperative term that dismisses them. They will not be interested in comments, because they are the true believers and the Al Qaeda's of the world know there are plenty of them out there—both inside and outside the United States.

As I have said previously, we are involved in a food fight within Islam that has been brewing for a century. From the founding of the Muslim Brotherhood in Egypt in the late 19th century, an element of Islam has rejected what it views as Western "modernism." This modernism is affecting the values of Islam, weakening it and thus diluting its practices and mores. Yet, those who espouse this message are willing to the use the 21st century battlefield of cyberspace to pursue their goals.

This enemy is a very different one than the current intelligence system is set up to confront—despite some obvious patches. With whatever modifications, the existing system was established to deal with the Soviet Union and nation-state enemies.

The West might argue over the motives of the past, but we knew what they were.

The grand game of Cold War spying was an easy one. They wanted code clerks. We wanted code clerks. They wanted top-level political information. We wanted the same. They wanted military secrets and so did we. If we caught each other's spies, we kicked them out of the country. A human chess game.

Ultimately, the leadership was a known commodity with Western-based ideals. And, after fifty years of practice, we had a well-developed spy system that still missed the rottenness of the system and the timing of its fall.

So, how do you collect information and disrupt an enemy whose ideology is not Western based? Who is convinced that death in the cause will afford paradise in an afterlife? How do you take on a non-nation state that exists in the ether of the Internet? You search it out where it exists and you find the enemy wherever they are—both abroad and at home.

STEP THREE: DOMESTIC INTELLIGENCE WILL BE MORE INTRUSIVE

We discussed earlier in the book the tradeoff between domestic intelligence and civil liberties. At various times in our history, we have been willing to impinge upon "normal rights" to protect our country in time of war. The time we live in now is like no other. And, sadly, the times call for more government intrusiveness in our lives.

In the case of the Civil War and World War II, we knew (or least thought) that there was a definitive time frame in which the rules would be imposed. A war was taking place; people were dying, and the homeland was threatened.

The Cold War was different. We faced a single, known enemy, but had no real idea how long the war would last. It wasn't even a war in the old sense of the word. It was a battle of wills over ideology.

We knew the Russians were unlikely to invade the United States, but we knew they might have spies in the United States who might engage in sabotage. We knew that these spies were also here to influence our politics or to steal our nuclear and other military secrets. Laws were passed including the Internal Security Act of 1950, otherwise known as the McCarran Act.

This act required that Communists register with the Attorney General and that a Subversive Activities Control Board "investigate persons suspected of engaging in subversive activities or otherwise promoting the establishment of a 'totalitarian dictatorship,' fascist or communist. Members of these groups could not become citizens, and in some cases, were prevented from entering or leaving the country. Citizen-members could be denaturalized in five years."[6]

It was on the back of this law and others, and the zeitgeist of the time, that the FBI carried on their investigations, eventually joined by CIA and the Army. The unregulated abuses were many, and the whole process was eventually discredited as we discussed earlier in the book.

It appears we are now in a state similar to the Cold War. The war against radical Islam as exemplified by Al Qaeda and the Taliban is likely to be a generational war. We are, however, going to be attacked in the United States. People have been and are going to be killed. We rejected the Cold War domestic spying as too intrusive, but still something needs to be done.

In Step Four, I will discuss the substantial expansion of American intelligence domestically with better internal coordination and reach out to the current intelligence gathering efforts of the United States. I take no joy in this. Still, we are faced with an enemy who wishes to kill us and take away our freedoms as we know them. They are a part of our population and can move about freely and unnoticed. Stretching the quote from Chairman Mao, we cannot allow these Islamic terrorists to swim about in the sea of regular Americans freely.

That being said, it is incumbent on all of us during this time to see that we are ever diligent over this expanded domestic intelligence. This is not lip service. This is a call to protect our civil liberties in a time of threat.

Fortunately, we do not live in the conformist 1950s anymore. Investigative journalists on the net and from the old media are the first responders for our freedoms. And, no matter what Americans think about the Congress, it is a place now much better turned to the oversight of civil liberties than it was 50 years ago when it was more a part of the problem than the solution.

One matter that is disturbing, however, is the current Administration's unwillingness to fill the seats on the Privacy and Civil Liberties Oversight Board. The Board was passed into law in 2007 based on recommendations from the 9/11 Commission.[7] The board itself is an advisory body/watchdog to assist the President of the United States and other senior executive branch officials in ensuring that concerns with respect to privacy and civil liberties are appropriately considered in the implementation of all laws, regulations, and executive branch policies related to the war against terrorism.[8] All five members have to undergo the Senate confirmation process. If confirmed, board members serve six-year terms.

The Obama Administration has yet to fill the positions of the committee for its tenure, as it appears to be examining the role of the group. In the meantime, the Congress wrote the Administration a letter in early April 2010 to "encourage [the Administration] to immediately nominate qualified individuals to the Privacy and Civil Liberties Oversight Board." The letter, signed by twenty-two Democratic House members, including House Homeland Security Chairman Bennie G. Thompson (D-MS), said, "Though both your fiscal year 2010 and 2011 budgets fund this Board, it is not operational."[9]

It is also incumbent on us as citizens to maintain vigilance over this new, more deeply intrusive intelligence structure. I am a firm believer in the American ideal of keeping government under control. Anyone who has seen the abuses of the past will know these are always possible at any time—either in the spirit of carrying out the law or for less honorable intentions.

I am particularly concerned about oversight of intelligence at the state and local levels. The ideas of collecting information and producing intelligence are good and helpful ones. However, local governments are not going to have the same capabilities to oversee the system, as seen with the federal oversight process. And look at how often they are wrong.

For the state and local authorities, I believe it is up to the federal government to mandate that the governors of the fifty states establish some kind of privacy oversight board or office. This could easily be an extension of their current state homeland security office and local legal authorities to monitor and report abuses in the system.

Let me also add that it is equally incumbent on the citizens of the United States to monitor and report on potential abuses. Obviously, the Internet, Web sites, and old media like newspapers are one way to get information out. But no matter what your political belief, I have an old-fashioned faith in organizations like the American Civil Liberties Union (ACLU) and the Federation of American Scientists (FAS) to get the truth out.

The ACLU web page says it right up front—they are opposed to:

> Illegal government spying, indefinite detention without charge or trial and government-sponsored torture programs after 9/11 transcended the bounds of law and our most treasured values in the name of national security. There has never been a more urgent need to restore individual freedoms, due process rights and our system of checks and balances.[10]

On the recent decision by the Obama Administration to consider removing Miranda rights from American citizens arrested on terrorist charges, Laura Murphy, Director of the ACLU Washington Legislative Office, said:

> President Obama has taken many important steps to restore respect for the Constitution and the rule of law, but his attorney general is now proposing that Congress chip away at the cherished Miranda protections. It's disappointing to hear Mr. Holder suggest that Americans should trade their freedoms for security. Congress should strongly reject this proposal and the underlying argument that the Constitution doesn't work. Gradually dismantling the Constitution will make us less free, but it will not make us more safe.[11]

Agree with it or not, this type of public oversight sets up a public debate that is crucial.

FAS is another example of such an important player. FAS was founded in 1945 by scientists who had worked on the Manhattan Project to develop the first atomic bombs. These scientists recognized that science had become central to many key public policy questions. They believed that scientists had a unique responsibility both to warn the public and policy leaders of potential dangers from scientific and technical advances and to show how good policy could increase the benefits of new scientific knowledge.[12]

Over the years, FAS has developed a Project on Government Secrecy, which "works to promote public access to government information and to illuminate the apparatus of government secrecy, including national security classification and declassification policies. The Project also publishes previously undisclosed or hard-to-find government documents of public policy interest, as well as resources on intelligence policy."[13]

STEP FOUR: A NEW INTELLIGENCE COMMUNITY

An ancient quote from the founder of Taoism, Lao Tzu, expresses it best: "If you do not change direction, you may end up where you are heading." Sadly, I believe the current organization of U.S. domestic intelligence collection is heading toward more mistakes and potential disasters. While bureaucratic organization often leads to glazed eyes and minds, it is the form by which we pursue the battle with our enemy. If we are not agile, if we fail to conform to his abilities, we will lose. In Vietnam, we played football while the enemy played soccer. We lost.

The intelligence system in the United States is based on an ancient document we have discussed, the National Security Act of 1947. It was added to over the years with various modifications that essentially approved additional large-scale organizations. It was perfectly suited to nation-state warfare. It adapted half-heartedly to non-nation state conflict.

The events of 9/11 were the result of a systematic intelligence failure. The system we developed and did not change substantially for nearly fifty years had neither flexibility nor the granularity for the job against Al Qaeda. Reactions to this, as we have discussed, were immediate patches. The October 2001 U.S.A. PATRIOT Act and the November 2002 Homeland Security Act gave the IC more flexibility in information sharing with the FBI and another layer of government with which to deal.

Finally, a half-hearted revamping occurred after the 9/11 Commission report recommendations and the Iraq WMD fiasco, when Congress and the president recognized that something needed to be done. The result, the 2004 Intelligence Reform and Terrorism Prevention Act, was based on an incomplete and sloppy bill from the Congress and baby steps from the White House produced the system with which we deal today. And it is not pretty or effective.

It is time that all three of these bills, now public laws, be reviewed by the Congress and the Executive Branch; call it a course correction in our battle. There is certainly precedent. The U.S. military was reformed a number of times during the Cold War, including the famous Goldwater-Nichols bill that revamped the Joint Chiefs, created joint fighting forces and solidified civilian control in the Pentagon.

FIRST, THINK LOCAL INTELLIGENCE

As I write this book in late May 2010, the failed bombing in Times Square has just taken place. A middle class Pakistani-American, Faisal Shazad, was angry at his life in America and sought out the Taliban to train with them for eight months. He returned to America, bought chemicals, propane, and firecrackers, and tried to light off a used pickup truck in the middle of the day surrounded by thousands of people. Fortunately, he was inept and the bomb did not go off.

Equally important, some observant citizens who saw the car belching smoke went to local cops on duty. They, in turn, called in the bomb squad, who dismantled the bomb. It took another two days to track down Shazad. Finally, it was an airport clerk with Emirates Airlines who noticed his name on the manifest list as the plane on which he was escaping was pulling out from the gate.

Shazad's capture was considered a success and was well spun in the press by both New York City government and the Obama Administration. The federal program was working. The New York City program was working. As John Stuart Mill once said, there is a kernel of truth in every statement. Let me note the other kernels missing from these self-congratulations.

From my standpoint, it is the "first responder" that made the difference. It was the person on the street and the local cop who did the job of stopping this bombing. It was an alert and informed citizenry that made the difference. And New York City should congratulate itself for the work it did to make that understanding a daily part of the New Yorker mentality.

As for the federal government, well, it tried. The FBI lost him in surveillance. Partial lists of names were passed around the air travel industry, but not to all airlines. Fortunately, an alert clerk was able to identify Shazad. Score one for the first responder and a half to the Feds.

The Shazad incident is the latest in a long line of examples of why the Washington, D.C., focus on itself and its local bureaucratic boxes is not working. There are some 17,600 local, state, and tribal police authorities. According to the U.S. Bureau of Labor Statistics, there are 684,000 police in the United States.[14], [15] They are our eyes and ears on the street and in our neighborhoods.

It is time for the federal government to stop looking inside the Beltway exclusively and begin to engage in serious domestic intelligence work with the locals.

The Feds will claim that some work is being done and support and information is being "passed down to the locals." They will talk about various grant programs to purchase needed equipment, like radios. They will note the seventy fusion centers around the country composed of local police and federal intelligence personnel on temporary assignment to them.

The Feds will also be happy to discuss the information systems they have established to provide data and information to all police departments—such as the Homeland Security Information Network. This network is a "comprehensive, nationally secure and trusted web-based platform able to facilitate 'Sensitive But Unclassified' information sharing and collaboration between federal, state, local, tribal, private sector, and international partners. [This] platform was created to interface with existing information-sharing networks to support the diverse 'Communities of Interest' engaged in preventing, protecting from, responding to, and recovering from all threats, hazards and incidents under the jurisdiction of the Department of Homeland Security."[16]

The reality is quite different. State and local authorities have been ignored or dismissed by the old IC. More often than not, you will hear the D.C. epithet that cops don't need to learn intelligence. They are law enforcement guys. They simply bust people. These old thinkers are simply wrong.[17]

We are a continental nation of 300 million people and 3.8 million square miles. The appropriate use and training of local police in both intelligence gathering and intelligence analysis would greatly enhance our capabilities to protect ourselves.

A program established by DHS's Intelligence and Analysis Bureau that provided standardized training programs throughout the country would provide a great leg up on the problem. Such a program should concentrate on how intelligence information is already part of what every policeman does, and how that information could be provided to specially trained analysts locally who could mix and match the information from other legal authorities, including from the Feds.

This system would also give the local police an opportunity to get their information in a comprehensive way back to the federal government intelligence services, who could incorporate it into their overall picture.

None of this can happen, however, without a comprehensive set of guidelines provided by the DHS for the targeting, use, storage, and access to this information. By connecting federal funding to these guidelines, we can make sure that we do not end up with police who push the line too far into our privacy and civil liberties.

MAKE THE FEDERAL INTELLIGENCE ORGANIZATIONS TRULY NATIONAL

The federal-level intelligence agencies must be able to face the realities of a new era in which there is little if any distinction between international and domestic. The basic legal framework is wrong and must be eliminated.

The Intelligence Reform and Terrorism Prevention Act of 2004, the legal basis of post 9/11 intelligence, must go. Congressional committees who did not know about either intelligence collection or analysis created the bill. Moreover, the Secretary of Defense at the time, Donald Rumsfeld, made sure that the authority of the DNI was neutered in terms of budget and program controls—the key to any success in Washington.

The DNI is not a director of anything, nor is the role national or really even intelligence. Instead of coordinating and directing the sixteen members of the IC, this role has been reduced to hectoring through small budget realignments and a barrage of questions issued by public statements of nearly 2,000 bureaucrats with no well-defined purpose. We need to either give the DNI the reins over the IC or return them to the CIA with strong legislation on how to coordinate community matters.

Second, the system of information sharing among the intelligence players is simply broken and must be fixed. Information is the lifeblood of intelligence and the basis of the analysis we must have to successfully deal with our enemy.

A security apparatus spawned in the 1950s, whose knee-jerk reaction is to classify material, imprisons the current system. Part of this does make sense as some information should not be shared freely or easily, but the assumption throughout the IC should not be that information is classified until proven otherwise.

This information-hoarding regime has been particularly irritating to the tens of thousands of state, local, and tribal first responders who neither need nor want a clearance. What these professionals need is usable information and analysis provided in a timely fashion. Information confined to "tear line" documents and analysis too highly classified to share outside the few does little good and in fact risks adding to the noise.

Edicts from such good people as Deputy DNI Mike Hayden, who said that the "need to share" outweighs the old system, is good thinking. However, the "iron majors" of the ancient regime have fought it tooth and nail. So far, they are winning. This only serves to discourage state and local people from sharing information—even if they knew what would do the folks in Washington any good.

So what needs to be done? I believe the entire revamping of the U.S. classification system is in order. The President's Intelligence Advisory Board or an outside group needs to take it on, set some reasonable guidelines, and then mandate through Executive Order what needs to be done and do it in less than a year—fast by government time.

It is further incumbent on the Executive Branch, the president in particular, to make sure the rules of the intelligence collection road are well defined. While no president likes to have his prerogatives circumscribed, no president can afford to have a public fearful of its government. The recent debate over FISA is but a whispering sample of what would happen if a large part of the American population discovered massive public databases collected on it with little regulation over storage, use, and access.

The president needs to be crystal clear to all the domestic intelligence players—at the national and local levels—that there is one set of rules to play by and those who violate those rules will be punished. Whether through Executive Order or through legislative agenda, the rules need to be debated and set for national and state and local authorities.

LAW ENFORCEMENT AND INTELLIGENCE TOGETHER

The third challenge to tackle is sticky but crucial to deal with as it is evolving quickly. This next challenge is the new type of intelligence collection and analysis needed by the intelligence "agencies" now in the game. The traditional IC has avoided dealing directly with law enforcement activities for a number of reasons: traditional focus on strategic goals and the public pranging they all took back in the 1970s for overly active involvement in domestic intelligence. That was then, this is now.

A number of people have proposed establishing an MI-5 to deal with the nexus of law enforcement and intelligence. Judge Posner has proposed a centralized MI-5 on a number of occasions and suggested folding the current National Security Division of the FBI into it.[18] We are too large a nation for that, our culture will not support it, and there are already too many moving parts to the puzzle.

But what are we to do as we are already partially pregnant on the issue of law enforcement and intelligence working together? The current seventy-plus fusion centers are leading the way for interaction between the old IC and some of the nation's state and local law enforcement authorities. However, they are only beginning to get the kind of guidance and understanding of collection and intelligence methods that they need.

A similar situation is also brewing in the area I like to call the new "domestic" IC. This IC is filled with agencies that have been made a part of the national security scene since 9/11 and need to collect tactical information to produce analysis for their customers within their individual agencies. The new IC consists of:

- Coast Guard (part of the other IC)
- Customs and Border Protection (CBP)
- Federal Emergency Management Agency (FEMA)
- Transportation Security Administration (TSA)
- U.S. Citizenship and Immigration Services (USCIS)
- U.S. Coast Guard

- U.S. Immigration and Customs Enforcement (ICE)
- U.S. Secret Service

This is a new kind of analysis being done by many who have never had any training and barely understand how the older IC works or how it can be tasked. The new IC is required to give its "policymakers"—agents in the field, officers on deck—information they can act upon or at least use to execute their duties.

Moreover, these analysts are being asked to move beyond the threat assessments and risk assessments of the traditional IC analyst. They are being asked to make recommendations to their policymakers on risk management. In short, they are being asked to lay out what resources should logically be thrown against a problem. Unlike their analytical cousins, they are being asked to make policy judgments and be policy proscriptive.

Honing this growing cadre and the work they do requires the kind of training and understanding of policy that they are getting only haphazardly right now. One can also understand why the problem is even greater at the state and local levels throughout the country. Even the fusion centers have an uneven record with CIA and FBI analysts trying to acquaint local analysts—most likely law enforcement professionals on the fly.

The solution to this problem lies in the revamping of the Homeland Security Act. The Homeland Security Act was a quick attempt to get all the players on homeland security together quickly. The FBI, with its usual aplomb, managed to escape the roundup with the claim that its primary focus remained white-collar crime. The addition of a huge National Security Division under the reauthorization of the 2006 U.S.A. PATRIOT has made the original argument laughable.

A NEW HEAD FOR DOMESTIC INTELLIGENCE AT THE FEDERAL LEVEL

The need for a proper mechanism that is adapted to America to do domestic intelligence collection and analysis is crucial. However, the MI-5 model will not work in the United States as there are at best too many law enforcement players spread over too large a field of play.

So what can the United States do to make domestic intelligence effective here? Provide ground rules for collection and analysis and set up proper mechanisms for exchanging that information. Well, we already have the place—the DHS's Office of Intelligence and Analysis.

We need to allow the Undersecretary of Intelligence for Homeland Security—currently long-time intelligence professional Caryn Wagner—to truly oversee the collection and analysis of domestic intelligence and its coordination with the rest of the IC. Let this person be the true Director for

Domestic Intelligence (DDI) and act as the "button hole" to the more traditional and internationally oriented IC.

This DDI's central control would allow a number of worthy changes and ideas. The DDI could provide a common training for intelligence collectors and analysts across the broad spectrum of national, state and local authorities.

Second, it would allow the federal government to truly control the flow of information between the federal government and state and local authorities. Classification systems could be made sensible. Rules regarding storage of information and sharing could be established, lending credibility and order to this lifeblood system.

Current Secretary of Homeland Security Janet Napolitano has already made some moves in that direction. For instance, The DHS is establishing a new office to coordinate its intelligence-sharing efforts in state and local intelligence fusion centers. Officials from different levels of government use information technology to share homeland security–related information through the centers.[19]

The new Joint Fusion Center Program Management Office will be part of DHS's Office of Intelligence and Analysis. It goals are to:

- Lead a DHS-wide effort to ensure non-federal law enforcement agencies can define what homeland security–related information they need and in what format they want it;
- Develop ways to assess threats and trends by gathering, analyzing, and sharing local and national information and intelligence through fusion centers;
- Coordinate with state, local, and tribal law enforcement leaders to ensure that DHS is providing the correct resources to fusion centers;
- Promote a sense of common mission and purpose at fusion centers through training and other support; and
- Develop and promote legal, privacy, civil rights, and civil liberties–related training and support to law enforcement partners and DHS employees.[20]

On this last area, it is crucial that the DDI interact with the private sector. This area of providing information and analysis has been quite sticky over the years due to self-imposed federal legal restrictions. Private industry has been frustrated trying to interact with the federal bureaucracy and has resorted to a self-created industry security system to gather and share information among them. While a DDI would not necessarily solve all the problems here, at least this person could interact more sensibly with those who own 85 percent of America's infrastructure as they "know the turf" better than the DNI.

Third, the DDI could reach out and exercise influence over the current outliers in the domestic intelligence sphere—the FBI's National Security Division and seventy separate and unguided fusion centers. It is unlikely they would submit to direct DDI control, but they would be better guided by a DDI focused on domestic intelligence rather than the more "distant" DNI.

Fourth, the DDI could coordinate the cyber war against Al Qaeda among the various homeland entities and act as chief "button hole." The multilayered bureaucracy developing for the cyber war is mind-boggling, including elements from the IC and the military with NSA in the lead—a witches' brew of bureaucrats fighting over their own turf. At least, a DDI could try to keep some kind of order in the domestic IC.

Fifth, the DDI would provide Congressional oversight with a single point of contact to go to regarding issues of the day, especially regarding the sharing of information and its use. Right now there is no central point of control for concerns about what kind of domestic intelligence is being collected and how it is used. The DDI could at least act as that first stop to see that guidance is being followed.

THE CONGRESS MUST DO ITS JOB AND SO MUST THE PRESIDENT

The last question begs discussion of at least two more nettlesome problems—Congressional oversight and the protection of personal liberties. On the first point, I am hardly going to be the first person to call for reform of oversight. But speaking as former Intelligence Counsel to two former Senate Majority Leaders, it is a mess and only the leadership can do anything about it. The mess is the number of committees overseeing the process of homeland security and its intelligence gathering and analysis.

The Executive Branch always complains when it comes to Congressional oversight. The complaints are as old as the Constitution itself. But the Congress holds the power of the purse, and the only way to get your program financed is "go to the Hill."

Well-executed oversight also provides the opportunity for a second set of eyes on the challenges of the Executive Branch—not that the latter will ever admit that to the Hill. It also fulfills the letter of the Constitution in that Congress is doing what it is supposed to do in terms of protecting the peoples' interests and seeing that their hard-earned money paid into the tax base is not squandered.

For issues of intelligence, the Senate Select Committee on Intelligence and its House brethren, the House Permanent Select Committee on Intelligence, are supposed to provide oversight for all intelligence matters, occasionally sharing military intelligence issues with the Senate and House Armed Services

Committees. It is not a totally workable system, however, as neither committee has been able to get a budget bill on the floor for years due to partisan bickering, but at least the oversight part is fairly controlled and well used. Domestic intelligence is another matter.

The Congressional oversight of Homeland Security is a tangled mess spread among eighty-six committees and subcommittees on the Hill. Vice Chairman of the 9/11 Commission, former Congressman Lee Hamilton said, "When you have oversight conducted by numerous committees and subcommittees, you tend not to get the rigor you need in oversight . . . the more [committees] you have engaged in the topic, the less robust it is. We think the executive branch needs very rigorous, independent oversight that can only really come from the Congress."[21]

As for the new IC, the situation is equally as bad. For example, the FBI's National Security Division efforts are under the Intelligence Committees. Their collection actions for law enforcement are under the Senate and House Judiciary Committee and all its subcommittees. Don't forget: they also report to both the Senate and House Homeland Security Committees.

I could continue on this issue, but the final point is this—you cannot have effective oversight of agencies and important domestic intelligence issues when so many committees are playing in the mix. From a practical standpoint, it is extraordinarily difficult to find staff that knows enough to be effective for each committee's use. It is also difficult to find people who are willing to submit to long and extensive background checks.

The bottom line is a simple but painful one—it is strictly up to the leadership of the Congress to decide who gets oversight of what. I truly understand that the power of oversight is not easily taken or redistributed on the Hill. These committee and subcommittee assignments are like hard currency: they buy you loyalty and are considered rewards.

THERE IS POLITICS ON CAPITOL HILL

As someone who has been in the Congressional "business" for over twenty years, I have heard the term "politicization of intelligence" thrown around more often than I care to remember. The accusation is usually thrown when someone dislikes someone else's conclusion using another IC analytical product.

However, the bitter debate in the last year over how an Administration informs the Hill about various intelligence activities has further muddied the already opaque waters. The incident in question was whether Speaker of House Nancy Pelosi was fully informed in 2002 by the Bush Administration of enhanced interrogation techniques at Guantanamo Bay, Cuba.

When questioned in July 2009, Pelosi said she was not provided a full briefing on the subject. A back-and-forth between Pelosi and the CIA took place. According to the CIA, while Pelosi was head of the House Intelligence Committee in 2002, she was told about enhanced interrogation techniques, including water boarding authorized for a captured terrorist, Abu Zubaydah in an hour-long briefing in 2002. After the briefing, Pelosi said she "was assured by lawyers with the CIA and the Department of Justice that the methods were legal."[22] The matter was eventually dropped with both sides claiming victory and with promises of more complete briefings by the Executive Branch to Hill leadership.

This is but one small example of how quickly an important and politically charged event can blow up into a scandal. That being said, and understanding the nature of the Hill being constantly under the pressure of raising money and running for office, I think we need to slow down when it comes to politicizing domestic intelligence. I know I am naïve on this issue. Congressional oversight is one thing, and a good one; taking offense for political stance does no one any good.

One final note of advice on Congressional oversight matters. I realize the intelligence committees in the eyes of many on the Hill have not covered themselves with glory—failing in many minds to detect the true problems of intelligence before 9/11 and allowing faulty intelligence estimates like the Iraq WMD to take place. But, at the very least, some committee must be given oversight.

It is time to recreate the Congressional oversight of intelligence. Given its importance both domestically and internationally, I suggest making a Joint Senate–House Select Committee. The leadership of both houses of the Congress would pick senior members of Foreign Relations, Judiciary, Armed Services, and Homeland Security Committees to serve on the committee.

This joint "super committee" should also take advantage of access to the General Accountability Office, which can provide the joint committee with expert personnel to conduct the kind of long-range studies on structure, personnel, and other over-the-horizon issues that current Committee staffs simply cannot accomplish.

JUST THE START

The journey of a thousand miles begins with the first step. We are likely in for a generation's worth of a fight with radical Islam—and expanded domestic intelligence. The rise of this amorphous enemy who reaches across cyberspace into our country and the minds of some of our people. I am secure, however, that while it took us a while to get our intelligence right for the Cold War, we'll do it again to include domestic intelligence.

And I am equally confident that, in the end, the federal government has the personnel and financial resources to deal with this threat. It will need to join with the state and local authorities to effectively manage this threat nationwide. This runs squarely into the American desire to keep the government out of its citizens' lives. The right-wing conspiratorial types will see the hand of Big Brother trying to reach out to them, but we have little choice.

As I have said, the vast number of state, local, and tribal police authorities prevents the United States from having anything that resembles a seamless system of information sharing. It also allows for potential abuses of the system that many justifiably fear. The regularization of information provision, sharing, and control via the federal government is the only way to deal with issue. Only the federal government can provide the kind of oversight that is necessary to do the job.

But remember, any enterprise this large and this complex is going to have some days better than others. No matter what openness there is in the process, no matter what structure is set up, there will be times when bad things happen. In the final analysis, the public must understand that risk management means just that—we can at best manage the risks involved from terrorism on our soil. We cannot prevent them, even if we were to spend all of our national treasures. Such is the nature of the beast. But we can block them, attack them at their roots, and wear them down with persistence.

And last, but hardly least, it is the challenge of maintaining the public's civil liberties in the midst of this maelstrom of analysis and information collection that matters most. While I touched on the issue earlier in the book, it is the stuff that encyclopedia volumes are made. Because I wanted to focus on the collection and analysis of domestic intelligence, I sidled away from the deeper intricacies of this most complex of issues.

Let me say this in the context of next steps. The strict regulation and oversight of domestic collection and analysis is crucial. Otherwise, all we are fighting for against an implacable enemy is lost. There are many emotional thoughts that can be put forth on this subject. For the purposes here, allow me to address only the bureaucratic ones.

One of the reasons I find the current system of Congressional oversight so appalling is that it is a misguided "court of appeal" for public injustices, a place where new rules can be made and old rules revised. The horrible mistakes of domestic intelligence were fostered because their actions grew in secrecy and there was no oversight. It is unlikely such an egregious set of actions would happen again in the same way. The problem is how they would happen in a different way.

In the final analysis, the success of domestic intelligence lies in the trust the American people have in a system that works to protect them. There will be bumps in the road and scandals, no doubt. But, we can ill afford not to have a workable system. And it must be one subject to access, debate, oversight, and evolutionary change when needed.

Notes

INTRODUCTION

1. Peter Greer, Christian Science Monitor, "Times Square Bomber Joins The Growing List of Inept Terrorists," www.csmonitor.com/USA/2010/0504/Times-Square-bomber-joins-the-growing-list-of-inept-terrorists, 4 May 2010.

2. Associated Press, "Underwear Bomber Doing Weapons Training in Yemen," http://www.huffingtonpost.com/2010/04/26/video-underwear-bomber-do_n_552899.html, 26 April 2010.

3. Al Baker and William Rashbaum, New York Times, "Police Find Bomb in Times Square," 1 May 2010, pg. 1.

4. William Rashbaum and Peter Baker, New York Times, "U.S. Arrests SUV Owner in Times Square Case," 4 May 2010, pg. 1.

5. Alex Spillius, U.K. Daily Telegraph, "Detroit Bomber: Obama Criticizes U.S. Intelligence Agencies," 5 Jan 2010, pg. 1.

6. Jake Tapper, ABCNews.com, "Director of National Intelligence Blair Responds to President's Comments," http://blogs.abcnews.com/politicalpunch/2010/01/director-of-national-intelligence-blair-responds-to-presidents-comments.html, 8 January 2010.

7. Walter Pincus, Washington Post, "Blair Discloses Budget For Intelligence Community," http://www.washingtonpost.com/wp-dyn/content/article/2009/09/16/AR2009091603208.html, 16 September 2009.

8. John Koehler, "*Stasi – The Untold Story of the East German Police*," Westview Press, 1999.

9. International Association of Chiefs of Police, http://discoverpolicing.org/why_policing/state, 2010.

10. U.S. Department of Homeland Security, http://www.dhs.gov/files/programs/gc_1156877184684.shtm, "State and Local Fusion Centers," 2010.

CHAPTER 1

1. Mark M. Lowenthal, Intelligence: From Secrets to Policy (Washington, DC: Congressional Quarterly Press, 2002 [second edition]), p. 8.

2. Jack Davis, "Defining the Analytic Mission: Facts, Findings, Forecasts and Fortunetelling," Studies in Intelligence, Special November 2002 Issue, p. 25–30.

3. Robert M. Clark, Intelligence Analysis: A Target-Centric Approach (2004, CQ Press)

4. Frank Cilluffo, Ronald A. Marks, George Salmoiraghi, "The Uses and Limits of U.S. Intelligence," The Washington Quarterly, Winter 2002, p. 61–74.

5. Ibid, p. 61.

6. Ibid, p. 72.

7. U.S. Central Intelligence Agency, The Central Intelligence Agency, Director of Intelligence Products, https://www.cia.gov/offices-of-cia/intelligence-analysis/products.html, 2010.

8. Final Report of the National Commission on Terrorist Attacks Upon the United States, "9/11 Commission Report, W.W. Norton, July 2004, p. 145–173.

9. Ibid.

10. Judge Richard Posner, "Remaking Domestic Intelligence," Hoover Institution Press, Stanford University, 2005, p. 1.

11. East Germany info, http://eastgermany.info/, 2010.

12. Richard Shears, "North Korean Man Executed for calling a friend in South Korea on mobile phone," U.K. Daily Mail, http://www.dailymail.co.uk/news/worldnews/article-1255375/North-Korean-man-executed-calling-friend-South-Korea-mobile-phone.html, 4 March 2010.

13. Eric Schmidt, President of Google, speech at National Advertisers Association, http://www.cnet.com/topic-news/eric-schmidt.html, October 8, 2005.

14. The Commission on the Capabilities of the United States Regarding Weapons of Mass Destruction, "WMD Report", Report to the President of the United States, U.S. Government Printing Office, 2005, p. 365.

15. Ibid, WMD Report, p. 367.

16. United States Code, Public Law 108–177, 17 December 2004.

17. U.S. Central Intelligence Agency, Clandestine Service, www.cia.gov/office-of-cia/clandestine-service, 2010.

18. Ibid, P.L. 108–177.

19. U.S. Director of National Intelligence, www.dni.org/what_collection, 2010.

20. Ibid.

21. U.S. Central Intelligence Agency, www.cia.gov, 2010.

22. Reed R. Probst, "Clausewitz on Intelligence," Studies in Intelligence (Fall 1985), 29–33.

23. Ton Hays and Sharon Theimer "Egyptian Agent Worked with Green Berets and Bin Laden," Jerusalem Post, 31 December 2001.

24. Mark Mazetti and Melissa Rubin, "Suicide Bomber Kills CIA Operatives," New York Times, http://www.nytimes.com/2010/01/01/world/asia/01afghan.html, 30 December 2009.

25. CNN.com, "Al Qaeda Tape of Alleged Suicide Bomber Who Killed Seven CIA Officers," http://www.cnn.com/2010/WORLD/asiapcf/04/30/afghanistan.al.qaeda.tape/index.html?iref=allsearch, 30 April 2010.

26. United States Code, Pub. L. No. 235, 80 Cong., 61 Stat. 496, 50 U.S.C. ch.15) and (P.L. 81–110, 63 Stat. 208).

27. President Harry S. Truman, National Security Council Intelligence Directive (NSCID) 9, www.whitehouse.gov, October 24, 1952.

28. Robert Louis Benson and Michael Warner, Editors, "*Venona – Soviet Espionage and the American Response*," National Security Agency and Central Intelligence Agency, 1996.

29. United States Code, Pub.L. 95–511, 92 Stat. 1783, enacted October 25, 1978, 50 U.S.C. 36.

30. President Ronald W. Reagan, Executive Order 12333, signed 4 December 1981, www.whitehouse.gov

31. Ibid, "Venona – Soviet Espionage and the American Response."

32. Loch Johnson, "*America's Secret Power*," Oxford University Press, 1989, pp. 133–156.

33. Ibid, pp. 234–255.

34. Ibid, 15 U.S.C. 36.

35. Gerald Posner, "*Why America Slept*," Ballantine Books, New York, September 2004.

36. Amy Zegart, Austin Long, Joshua Rovner, ed., *How Intelligent Is Intelligence Reform?* International Security - Volume 30, Number 4, Spring 2006, pp. 196–208.

37. Frank Cilluffo, Ronald Marks, and George Salmoiraghi, "The Uses and Limits of U.S. Intelligence," Washington Quarterly, Winter 2002.

38. The Definition of the Internet, Wikipedia, http://en.wikipedia.org/wiki/Internet, 29 April 2010.

CHAPTER 2

1. Jack Davis, "Defining the Analytical Mission: Facts, Findings, Forecasts and Fortunetelling," Studies in Intelligence, Special November 2002 Issue, 25–30.

2. U.S. Department of Homeland Security, DHS.org, National Infrastructure Protection Plan, http://www.dhs.gov/files/programs/editorial_0827.shtm, 2010.

3. DHS, National Strategy of the Physical Protection of Critical Infrastructures (February 2003), www.dhs.gov/files/programs, 2010.

4. Ibid, DHS.org, National Infrastructure.

5. Ibid.

6. Ibid.

7. Ibid.

8. Former Assistant Secretary of Homeland Security, Infrastructure Protection, the Hon. Robert Liscouski, Interview, 9 April 2010.

9. Ibid, DHS 2009 Infrastructure Protection Plan.

10. Ibid.

11. Information Sharing and Analysis Center Councils, http://www.isaccouncil.org/, 2010.

12. Former Special Assistant to the President for Homeland Security Frank Cilluffo, Interview, 4 April 2010.

13. U.S. Director of National Intelligence, "Annual Threat Assessment of the United States Intelligence Community for 2010", www.dni.gov/testimonies/20100202_testimony.pdf2, February 2010.

14. Ibid.

15. Ibid.

16. Ibid.

17. Mark Mazzetti, "Senators Warned of U.S. Terror Attack By July," New York Times, http://www.nytimes.com/2010/02/03/us/politics/03intel.html, 3 February 2010.

18. James Carafano, "30 Terrorist Plots Foiled," Eurasia Review, http://www.eurasiareview.com/201006062758/30-terrorist-plots-foiled-how-the-system-worked.html, 30 April 2010.

19. Ibid.

20. Robert Spencer, "Alleged Coconspirator Testifies at Virginia Jihad Trial." *Jihad Watch*, http://www.jihadwatch.org/2004/02/alleged-coconspirator-testifies-at-virginia-jihad-trial.html, 12 Feb. 2004.

21. Mary Beth Sheridan, "Hardball Tactics in an Era of Threats." *The Washington Post.* http://www.washingtonpost.com/wp-dyn/content/article/2006/09/02/AR2006090201096.html, 3 September 2006.

22. Ibid.

23. Declan Walsh, "The Mystery of Dr. Aafia Siddiqui," The Manchester (U.K.) Guardian, http://www.guardian.co.uk/world/2009/nov/24/aafia-siddiqui-al-qaida, 24 November 2009.

24. Scott Shane, and Elizabeth Bushmiller, "Pentagon Report on the Ft. Hood Shooting Details Failures," New York Times, http://www.nytimes.com/2010/01/16/us/politics/16hasan.html 15 January 2010.

25. Scott, Shane, "U.S. Approves Targeted Killing of American Cleric," New York Times, http://www.nytimes.com/2010/04/07/world/middleeast/07yemen.html 6 April 2010.

26. Mark Lowenthal, "Let's Not Become Our Own Worst Enemy," McClatchy Newspapers, http://www.mcclatchydc.com/2010/01/13/82268/commentary-lets-not-become-our.html, 13 Jan. 2010.

27. Paul Campos, "Undressing the Terror Threat," Wall Street Journal, http://online.wsj.com/article/SB10001424052748704130904574644651587677752.html, 9 Jan 2010.

28. Fareed Zakaria, "Don't Panic," Newsweek, http://www.newsweek.com/2010/01/08/don-t-panic.html, 9 Jan 2010.

29. Ibid, Campos.

30. Mark Thiessen, "*Courting Disaster: How the CIA Kept America Safe and How Barack Obama Is Inviting the Next Attack*," Regnery Publishing, 2010.

31. Ibid.

32. Ibid.

33. George Michael, "*Adam Gadahn and the Al Qaeda Internet Strategy*," Middle East Policy, Fall 2009, 135.

34. Ibid, Zakaria.

CHAPTER 3

1. U.S. Constitution, Articles I, II, III and IV.

2. Ibid.

3. Ibid.

4. Ibid.

5. Ernst Volkman, "*Espionage: The Greatest Spy Operations of the Twentieth Century,*" Wiley Publications, 1996.

6. U.S. Espionage Act, enacted 15 June 1917, http://codes.lp.findlaw.com/uscode/18/I/37/793.

7. The Sedition Act of 1918, enacted 16 May 1918 http://wwi.lib.byu.edu/index.php/The_U.S._Sedition_Act.

8. Ibid, Espionage Act of 1917.

9. Ibid, Sedition Act of 1918.

10. Avrich, Paul, "*Sacco and Vanzetti: The Anarchist Background,*" Princeton University Press, 1991, p. 91.

11. Chris Finan, "*From the Palmer Raids to the Patriot Act: A History of the Fight for Free Speech in America,*" Beacon Press, 2008.

12. Ronald Kessler, "Bureau: The Secret History of the FBI," St. Martin's Press, 2003.

13. Robert B. Stinnett. "Day of Deceit: The Truth about FDR and Pearl Harbor," Touchstone, paperback ed. 2001.

14. Thomas F. Troy, (1993-09-22). "Truman on the CIA," https://www.cia.gov/library/center-for-the-study-of-intelligence/csi-publications/books-and-monographs/our-first-line-of-defense-presidential-reflections-on-us-intelligence/truman.html, 2010.

15. Letters to President Truman, CIA Library, www.cia.gov/library, 2010.

16. United States Code, "The National Security Act of 1947," 50 U.S.C. 15.

17. United States Code, "CIA Act of 1948," P.L. 81–110.

18. Robert Benson and Michael Warner, ed., "Venona: Soviet Espionage and the American Response 1939–1957," National Security Agency and Central Intelligence Agency, 1996.

19. Sam Roberts, "*The Brother: the untold story of the Rosenberg Case.*" Random House Inc., 2003.

20. Loch Johnson, "*America's Secret Power,*" Oxford University Press, 1989.

21. Ibid.

22. Ibid.

23. Ibid.

24. David Frum, "*How We Got Here: The '70s.*" New York, New York: Basic Books. 1990, pp. 49–51.

25. Senate Select Committee on Intelligence was established by S. Res. 400, 19 May 1976 and the House Permanent Select Committee on Intelligence, H.R.458, 14 July 1977.

26. President Gerald R. Ford, Executive Order 11905, 16 February 1976.

27. President James Earl Carter, Executive Order 12036, 28 January 1978.

28. United States Code, "Foreign Intelligence Surveillance Act," 50 U.S.C. 36, October 1978.

29. President Ronald W. Reagan, Executive Order 12333, 4 December 1981.

30. Final Report of the National Commission on Terrorist Attacks Upon the United States (The 9/11 Commission), W.W. Norton, 27 May 2004.

31. Ibid.

32. Ibid.

33. United States Code, "U.S.A PATRIOT Act," P.L 107–56.

34. United States Code, "Posse Commitatus Act," 18 U.S.C. 1385.

35. United States Code, "Insurrection Act of 1807," 10 U.S.C. 331.

36. United States Code, "Homeland Security Act (HSA) of 2002," Pub. L. No. 107–296.

37. United States Code, "The Aviation Security Act," Pub L. No. 107–71.

38. U.S. Transportation and Safety Administration, www.tsa.gov/what_we_do, 2010.

39. U.S. TSA Customs and Border Patrol, www.tsa/cbp.gov, 2010.

40. U.S. TSA, www.tsa/cbp/cgov/border_security, 2010.

41. Ibid, www.cbp.gov.

42. Ibid.

43. United States Code, "The Secure Fence Act of 2006" Public Law 109–367.

44. Randal Archibold, "Budget Cut for Fence on U.S.-Mexican Border," New York Times, http://www.nytimes.com/2010/03/17/us/17fence.html, 16 March 2010.

45. Hilary Hilton, "Opponents of Mexican Fence Look to Obama," Time.com, http://www.time.com/time/nation/article/0,8599,1872650,00.html, 21 January 2009.

46. Ibid, www.cbp.gov.

47. U.S. Department of Homeland Security, www.dhs.gov/xnews/releases, 27 March 2008.

48. Ellen Nakashima, "Electronic Passports Raise Privacy Issues," Washington Post, http://www.washingtonpost.com/wp-dyn/content/article/2007/12/31/AR20071231019 22.html, 1 January 2008.

49. Michele Malkin, "Go-Fly List Endangers Public," Harrisonburg, VA Daily Record, http://www.dailynews-record.com/archive_details.php?AID=47039&CH=Opinion &SUB=Op-Ed:%20Viewpoint&type=week, 11 May 2010.

50. Shane Harris, "*The Watchers: The Rise of America's Surveillance State*," Speech in Portland, Oregon, 3 March 2010.

51. Eileen Sullivan, "Travelers to U.S. Face New Terror Screening Checks," Associated Press, http://www.aolnews.com/category/nation/?expired=true, 2 April 2010.

52. Ted Barrett, "Kennedy Has Company on Airline Watchlist," CNN.com, http://www.cnn.com/2004/ALLPOLITICS/08/20/lewis.watchlist/, 20 August 2004.

53. Barry Steinhardt, "Terrorist Watch List Hits One Million Names," Huffington Post.com, http://www.huffingtonpost.com/barry-steinhardt/terrorist-watch-list-hits _b_112596.html, 14 July 2008.

54. American Civil Liberties Union, www.ACLU.org/technology-and-liberty/ terrorwatch, 2010.

55. Robert O'Harrow, "Centers Tap Into Personal Databases," Washington Post, http://www.washingtonpost.com/wp-dyn/content/article/2008/04/01/ AR2008040103049.html, 2 April 2008.

56. Ibid.

57. Ibid.

CHAPTER 4

1. U.S. Central Intelligence Agency, www.cia.gov/history, 2010.

2. U.S. Director of National Intelligence, www.dni.gov, 2010.

3. U.S. Federal Bureau of Investigation, http://www.fbi.gov/contact/fo/fo.htm, "Your Local Field Office."

4. *Time Magazine*, "The Bombshell Memo," http://www.time.com/time/covers/ 1101020603/memo.html, 21 May 2002.

5. FBI Director Robert Mueller, Congressional Testimony, Senate Judiciary Committee, 25 March 2009.

6. Former Assistant Secretary of Infrastructure, Department of Homeland Security Robert Liscouski, Personal Interview, 7 April 2010.

7. CNN.com, "Baltimore Tunnel Reopens After Threat," 18 October 2005.

8. Ibid.

9. Craig Horowitz, New York Magazine.com, "The NYPD War on Terror," http://nymag.com/nymetro/news/features/n_8286/, April 2010.

10. Ibid.

11. Former Assistant to the President for Homeland Security, Preparedness, Daniel Kaniewski, Personal Interview, 6 April 2010.

12. Ibid and Electronic Privacy Information Center, "Information Fusion Centers and Privacy," June 2008.

13. Ibid, Kaniewski.

14. Paul Parformak, Congressional Research Service, "*Guarding America: Security Guards and U.S. Critical Infrastructure Protection*," 12 November 2004.

15. Daniel Dombey, "Interview with Secretary of State Hillary Clinton — Agencies Ill-Armed to Fight US-Based Terrorists", http://www.state.gov/secretary/rm/2010/04/ 143100.htm, *Financial Times*. 16 Jan 2010.

16. Ibid.

17. Gregg Carlstrom, "Connecting Agencies: Can Obama End Mistrust in Intel Community?" *Federal Times*. http://www.federaltimes.com/article/20100110/ AGENCY04/1100308/-1/RSS, 10 Jan 2010.

18. Government Computer News, "Major IT Problems Remain the Same, Survey Reports," http://gcn.com/Articles/2009/03/03/CIO-survey-Tech-America.aspx, 3 March 2009.

19. Ibid.

20. Eric Lichtblau, "FBI Faces Setback in Computer Overhaul," New York Times, http://www.nytimes.com/2010/03/19/us/19fbi.html, 18 March 2010.

21. Ibid, Federal Times, 10 Jan 2010.

22. Bobby Ghosh, "Spotlight: the Intelligence Breakdown." *Time Magazine.* http://www.time.com/time/magazine/article/0,9171,1952333,00.html, 10 Jan 2010.

23. Mark M. Lowenthal, "Commentary: Let's Not Become Our Own Worst Enemy." *McClatchy Newspapers.* http://www.mcclatchydc.com/2010/01/13/82268/commentary-lets-not-become-our.html, 13 Jan 2010.

24. Ibid.

25. Doyle McManus, "Connecting the Intelligence Dots Will Require Clout." http://articles.latimes.com/2010/jan/10/opinion/la-oe-mcmanus10-2010jan10, *Los Angeles Times.* 10 Jan 2010.

26. Richard Posner, "*Preventing Surprise Attacks.*" Stanford: Hoover Institution, 2005, 103.

27. Ibid, 141.

28. Robert Jervis, "Think Different, CIA." *Boston Globe.* Jervis, Robert. http://www.boston.com/bostonglobe/ideas/articles/2010/01/17/think_different_cia/, 17 Jan 2010.

29. Sebastian Rotella, "U.S. Learned Intelligence on Airline Bomb Suspect While he was En Route." *Los Angeles Times.* http://articles.latimes.com/2010/jan/06/nation/la-naw-airline-terror7-2010jan07, 6 Jan 2010.

30. Tim Starks, "Terrorism Briefings Prompt Questions on Technology, Information-Sharing." *Congressional Quarterly,* http://halrogers.house.gov/News/DocumentSingle.aspx?DocumentID=166699, 14 Jan 2010.

31. Hsu, Spencer S. and Karla Adam, "International Cooperation a Challenge for Air Security." *Washington Post.* 9 Jan 2010.

32. Posner, Richard, "*Remaking Domestic Intelligence*". Stanford: Hoover Institution, 2005, 18.

33. Spencer S. Hsu, and Karla Adam, "International Cooperation a Challenge for Air Security." *Washington Post,* http://www.washingtonpost.com/wp-dyn/content/article/2010/01/08/AR2010010803696.html, 9 Jan 2010.

34. Ibid.

35. Ibid.

36. Gregg Carlstrom, "Connecting Agencies: Can Obama End Mistrust in Intel Community?" *Federal Times,* http://www.federaltimes.com/article/20100110/AGENCY04/1100308/-1/RSS, 10 Jan 2010.

37. Ben Worthen, "Private Sector Keeps Mum on Cyber Attacks." *Wall Street Journal,* http://online.wsj.com/article/SB10001424052748704541004575011113352790040.html, 18 Jan. 2010.

38. Ibid.

39. Ibid.

40. Posner, Richard, "*Remaking Domestic Intelligence,*" Stanford: Hoover Institution, 2005, 3.

41. Ibid, 3.

42. Ibid, 58.

43. "September 11 and the Imperative of Reform in the U.S. Intelligence Community: Additional Views of Senator Richard C. Shelby, Vice Chairman, Senate Select Committee on Intelligence," Dec. 10, 2002, 62–63.

44. Richard Posner, *Remaking Domestic Intelligence*. Stanford: Hoover Institution, 2005, 15.

45. Ibid, 16.

46. William E. Odom, "Why the FBI Can't Be Reformed." *Washington Post*. http://www.washingtonpost.com/wp-dyn/content/article/2005/06/28/AR2005062801 249.html29, June 2005.

47. Andrea Elliott, "You Can't Talk to an FBI Agent That Way, or Can You?" *New York Times*, http://www.nytimes.com/2005/06/04/nyregion/04muslim.html, 4 June 2005.

48. Richard Posner "*Remaking Domestic Intelligence*." Stanford: Hoover Institution, 2005. 23.

49. Robert Ackerman, "Washington D.C. Police Confront Homeland Security Challenges," *AFCEA Signal Magazine*, February 2010, p. 18.

50. Ibid.

51. Ibid.

52. The United States Military District of Washington, www.mdw.army.mil/jfhq-ncr, 2010.

53. Ibid.

54. National Capitol Region Homeland Security Program, www.ncrhomeland security.org/overview, 2010.

55. Ibid, www.ncrhomelandsecurity.org/overview.

CHAPTER 5

1. Richard Posner, "We Need Our Own MI-5," Op-ed, *Washington Post*, http://www.washingtonpost.com/wp-dyn/content/article/2006/08/14/AR2006081401160.html, 15 August 2006.

2. Ibid.

3. Final Report of the National Commission on Terrorist Attacks Upon the United States (9/11 Commission Report), remarks of former MI-5 head Stella Rimington.

4. United Kingdom Security Service (MI-5) web site, www.mi5.gov.uk.

5. United Kingdom Common Law, The Police Act of 1996, 1996, Chapter 16.

6. Bruce Hoffman, Rand Corporation Counterterrorism Expert, Testimony before U.S. Senate Foreign Relations Committee, 18 July 2006.

7. The Official Secrets Act of 1889 of the United Kingdom, (as modified), 52&53 Vict.52.

8. The Official Secrets Act of 1989, c.6.

9. Ibid.

10. Tom Kelly, "Big Brother Britain Has More CCTV Cameras Than China," U.K. Daily Mail, http://www.dailymail.co.uk/news/article-1205607/Shock-figures-reveal-Britain-CCTV-camera-14-people—China.html, 11 August 2009.

11. Interview with Dr. David Young, CEO, Oxford Analytica, 6 April 2010.

12. United Kingdom Anti-Terrorism Crime and Security Act of 2001, c.24.

13. United Kingdom Prevention of Terrorism Act of 2005, c.2.

14. Hugh Muir and Rose Cowan, "Four bombs in 50 minutes, Britain suffers its worst ever terror attack," *The Guardian*, 8 July 2005, 1.

15. Ibid.

16. The Times On Line, "Police Snipers Track Al-Qaeda Suspects," http://www.timesonline.co.uk/tol/news/uk/article544971.ece, 17 July 2005.

17. BBC.com, "Man Shot Not Connected to Bombing," http://news.bbc.co.uk/2/hi/4711021.stm, 23 July 2005.

18. BBC.com, "Police Guilty over Menezes Case," http://news.bbc.co.uk/2/hi/uk_news/7069796.stm, 1 November 2007.

19. Todd Masse, Congressional Research Service, "*Domestic Intelligence in the United Kingdom: Applicability of the MI-5 Model to the United States*," May 19, 2003.

20. Ibid, Masse, CRS, 1.

CHAPTER 6

1. John Locke, "*Two Treatises of Government*," 1689.

2. *Terminello v. Chicago*, U.S. Supreme Court, 337 U.S. 1, 1949.

3. Abraham Lincoln, Presidential Order Suspending Habeus Corpus, http://usgovinfo.about.com/od/historicdocuments/a/lincolnhabeas.htm, 24 September 1862.

4. Ibid.

5. Civil-liberties.com,   http://www.civil-liberties.com/pages/did_lincoln.htm, "Was Habeas Corpus Ever Suspended.

6. United States Code, 42 U.S.C. 1981.

7. United States Code, 42 U.S.C. 1983.

8. Ibid.

9. President Franklin D. Roosevelt, Executive Order 9066, 19 Feb 1942.

10. U.S. Supreme Court, *Korematsu v. U.S.*, 323 U.S. 214, (1944).

11. Ibid, *Korematsu v. U.S.*

12. The Aviation and Tranportation Security Act, Pub. Law 107–71, 19 November 2001.

13. USA PATRIOT ACT (*Uniting and Strengthening America by Providing Appropriate Tools Required to Intercept and Obstruct Terrorism Act of 2001*) (P. L. 107–56), 26 October 2001.

14. Summary of USA PATRIOT ACT, http://en.wikipedia.org/wiki/USA_ PATRIOT_Act, Wikipedia.

15. Ibid.

16. Ibid.

17. Ibid.

18. President George W. Bush, Executive Order 13354, http://www.fas.org/irp/offdocs/eo/eo-13354.htm, 1 May 2003.

19. U.S. National Counterterrorism Center, www.nctc.gov, 2010.

20. President William Clinton, Presidential Decision Directive 75, http://www.fas
.org/irp/offdocs/pdd/pdd-75.htm, 5 January 2001.

21. U.S. Department of Defense, DOD Directive 5105.67, dated 19 February 2002.

22. John Solomon and Carrie Johnson, "FBI Broke Laws For Years in Phone
Record Search," Washington Post, 18 Jan 2010.

23. Shane Harris, "*The Watchers: The Rise of America's Surveillance State*,"
Penguin Press, 2010, p. 172.

24. Ibid, "The Watchers."

25. Ibid, "The Watchers."

26. Leslie Cauley, "NSA Has Massive Databases of American Phone Calls," USA
Today, 11 May 2006.

27. Ibid.

28. Andrew Bamford, "Echelon Spy Network Revealed," BBC, http://news.bbc
.co.uk/2/hi/503224.stm, 3 November 1999.

29. Ibid, BBC and Declan Mccullough and Anne Broache, CNET News, "NSA
Eavesdropping: How It Might Work," http://news.cnet.com/NSA-eavesdropping-
How-it-might-work/2100-1028_3-6035910.html, 7 November 2006.

30. European Parliament: Temporary Committee on the ECHELON Interception
System "*On the existence of a global system for the interception of private and commercial communications (ECHELON interception system)*," 7 November 2001.

31. James Bamford, "*Body of Secrets*," Anchor Books, 2002.

32. The Pinkerton Company, www.pinkertons.com and Kroll Associates,
www.kroll.com.

33. Peter Lewis, "Companies Turn To Private Spies," Fortune Magazine, http://
money.cnn.com/magazines/fortune/fortune_archive/2004/08/23/379380/index.htm,
23 August 2004.

34. Ibid.

35. Ibid.

36. Ibid.

37. Electronic Privacy Information Center (EPIC), www.epic.org/privacy/
choicepoint.

38. www.choicepoint.com.

39. United States Code, "Privacy Act of 1974," 5 U.S.C. 552a.

40. United States Code, "Computer Matching and Privacy Protection Act of
1988," 5 U.S.C. 552a (o).

41. Privacilla.org, www.privacilla/org/government/privacyact, 2010.

42. U.S. Congress, General Accountability Office Report, "Personal Information:
Key Federal Privacy Laws Do Not Require Information Resellers to Safeguard All
Sensitive Data," June 2006.

43. Ibid.

44. Marc A. Theissen, "*Courting Disaster: How the CIA Made America Safe
and How the Obama Administration Is Inviting the Next Attack*," Regnery Press, 18
January 2010.

45. PBS.org, "Spying on the Home Front," Interview with Suzanne Spaulding, 15
May 2007.

46. "President Obama Directs the National Security and Homeland Security Advisors to Conduct Immediate Cyber Security Review." *The White House Press Office* 2009-02-09.

47. John Broder, "Clinton Readies New Approach on Smut," New York Times, http://www.nytimes.com/1997/06/27/us/clinton-readies-new-approach-on-smut.html, 27 June 1997.

48. Scott Shane and Squad Mekhennet, "From Condemning Terror to Preaching Jihad," http://www.nytimes.com/2010/05/09/world/09awlaki.html, New York Times, 9 May 2010.

49. Evgeny Morosov, "Battling the Cyberwarmongers," http://online.wsj.com/article/SB10001424052748704370704575228653351323986.html, Wall Street Journal, 8 May 2010.

50. Nathan Hodge, "Prospective U.S. Cyber Commander Talks Terms of Digital Warfare," www.wired.com, http://www.wired.com/dangerroom/2010/04/pentagons-prospective-cyber-commander-talks-terms-of-digital-warfare/, 15 April 2010.

51. Ibid, USA PATRIOT Act.

52. Kim Zetter, "NSA Dominance of Cyber security Would Lead to 'Grave Peril', Ex-Cyber Chief Tells Congress," www.wired.com, http://www.wired.com/threatlevel/2009/03/nsa-dominance-o/, 10 March 2009.

53. Siobhan Gorman, "New Military Command To Focus on Cyber security," Wall Street Journal, 22 April 2009, 1.

54. William Jackson, "DOD Creates Cyber Command as U.S. Strategic Command Sub-Unit," Federal Computer Week, http://fcw.com/articles/2009/06/24/dod-launches-cyber-command.aspx, 24 June 2009.

55. Ibid.

56. Jason Miller, "DOD Cyber Command Will Take a Defensive Posture," Federal News Radio, http://www.federalnewsradio.com/?sid=1935637&nid=35, 16 April 2010.

57. Kim Ketter, "Obama Says Cyber Czar Won't Spy On The Net," www.wired.com; 29 May 2009.

58. U.S. Supreme Court, *Miranda v. Arizona*, 26 U.S. 436 (1966).

59. Wikipedia, "*Miranda v. Arizona*," http://en.wikipedia.org/wiki/Miranda_warning, 2010.

60. James Risen and Phillip Shenon, "U.S. Says It Stopped Al Queda Plot to Use Radioactive Bomb," New York Times, 10 June 2002.

61. *Padilla v. C.T. Hanft*, U.S. Supreme Court, Refusal Writ of Certiori, 3 April 2006.

62. U.S. Supreme Court, *Hamedi v. Rumsfeld*, 527 U.S. 507 (2004).

63. Senator John McCain, "The Don Imus Show, Interview," 4 May 2010, Fox Business Network.

CHAPTER 7

1. U.S. Commission on National Security/21st Century (Hart-Rudman Commission), "Roadmap for National Security, Imperative for Change," http://www.au.af.mil/au/awc/awcgate/nssg/, February 2001.

2. FindLaw.com, The President Daily Brief, "Bin Laden Determined to Strike in the U.S.," http://news.findlaw.com/hdocs/docs/terrorism/80601pdb.html, 6 August 2001.

3. Peter Bergen, "The Osama Bin Laden I Know," *Free Press*, January 2006, p. 75.

4. Richard Posner, "Our Domestic Intelligence Crisis," *Washington Post*, http://www.washingtonpost.com/wp-dyn/content/article/2005/12/20/AR2005122001053.html, 21 December 2005.

5. Mark Levitt, "Preparing for the Next Terrorist," Politico.com, http://dyn.politico.com/members/forums/thread.cfm?catid=1&subcatid=4&threadid=4032773, 10 May 2010.

6. Internal Security Act of 1950, 50 U.S.C. 781.

7. P.L. 110–53, 3 August 2007.

8. Roger Z. George, Robert D. Kline (2005). "*Intelligence and the National Security Strategist*." Rowan & Littlefield, 572.

9. Mathew Harwood, "House Lawmakers Tell Obama To Fill Civil Liberties Posts," Security Management Magazine, http://www.securitymanagement.com/news/house-lawmakers-tell-obama-fill-civil-liberties-board-006979, 1 April 2010.

10. The American Civil Liberties Union, http://www.aclu.org/national-security, 2010.

11. Ibid.

12. The Federation of American Scientists, http://www.fas.org/, 2010.

13. Ibid.

14. United State Department of Labor, www.bls.gov/oco, 2010.

15. Ibid, "and another 120,000 law enforcement officers in the Federal government."

16. United States Department of Homeland Security, www.dhs.gov/files/program/gc_1156888108137.shtw, 2010.

17. Judge Richard Posner, "*Remaking Domestic Intelligence*," Hoover Institution Press, July 2005, p. 7.

18. Ibid, Posner, "*Remaking Domestic Intelligence*."

19. Ben Bain, Federal Computer Week, "DHS Establishes Office for Intelligence Sharing Centers," http://fcw.com/articles/2009/09/30/web-new-dhs-fusion-center-office.aspx, 30 September 2009.

20. Ibid.

21. Lee Hamilton, Speech on Homeland Security, The Center for Public Integrity, Washington, D.C., 7 July 2009.

22. Jody Warrick and Dan Evans, "Hill Briefed on Water boarding in 2002," http://www.washingtonpost.com/wp-dyn/content/article/2007/12/08/AR2007120801664.html, Washington Post, 9 September 2007.

Bibliography

Andrew, Christopher. *For the President's Eyes Only—Secret Intelligence and the American Presidency from Washington to Bush.* New York: Harper Perennial, 1996.

Bamford, James. *The Puzzle Palace—Inside the National Security Agency, America's Most Secret Intelligence Organization.* New York: Penguin, 1983.

Gentry, Curt. *J. Edgar Hoover—The Man and the Secrets.* New York: W.W. Norton and Company, 2001.

George, Roger, and Kline, Robert, eds. *Intelligence and the National Security Strategist: Enduring Issues and Challenges.* Washington DC: National Defense University, 2004.

Harris, Shane. *The Watchers—The Rise of America's Surveillance State.* New York: Penquin Press, 2009.

Johnson, Loch, and Wirtz, James, eds. *Intelligence and National Security—The Secret World of Spies (An Anthology).* New York: Oxford University Press, 2007.

Kessler, Ron. *The Secret History of the FBI.* New York: St. Martin's Paperbacks, 2003.

Lane, Frederick S. *American History—A Four Hundred Year History of Our Most Contested Right.* Boston, MA: Beacon Press, 2009.

Lowenthal, Mark. *Intelligence from Secrets to Policy.* Thousand Oaks, CA: CQ Press, 2008.

Sims, Jennifer E., and Gerber, Burton, eds. *Transforming U.S. Intelligence.* Washington DC: Georgetown University Press, 2005.

Slobogin, Christopher. *Privacy at Risk—The New Government Surveillance and the Fourth Amendment.* Chicago: University of Chicago Press, 2007.

The 9/11 Commission. *Final Report of the National Commission on Terrorist Attacks Upon the United States.* New York: W.W. Norton and Company, 2003.

The Commission on the Intelligence Capabilities of the United States Regarding
    Weapons of Mass Destruction. *Report to the President of the United States.*
    Washington DC: U.S. Government Printing Office, 2005.
Zegart, Amy. *Spying Blind—The FBI, the CIA, and the Origins of 9/11.* Princeton,
    NJ: Princeton University Press, 2009.

Index

About the Author

RONALD A. MARKS spent 16 years at the Central Intelligence Agency as both a clandestine services officer and a Congressional liaison to five Directors of CIA. He served as Intelligence Counsel to Senate Majority Leaders Robert Dole and Trent Lott.

Currently, Marks is a Senior Fellow at the George Washington University Homeland Security Policy Institute where he acts as an expert on domestic intelligence and other security issues. He is also Adjunct Professor for Intelligence and National Security at the National Defense University's College of International Security Affairs where he teaches graduate level courses in homeland security and intelligence.

Marks has written and commented extensively on homeland security issues in the press and academic journals including C-SPAN's Washington Journal, Fox News and the Washington Quarterly. In additional to lecturing on intelligence issues around the country, Marks writes weekly commentaries for the National Journal's Experts blog on National Security.